Hans Broek

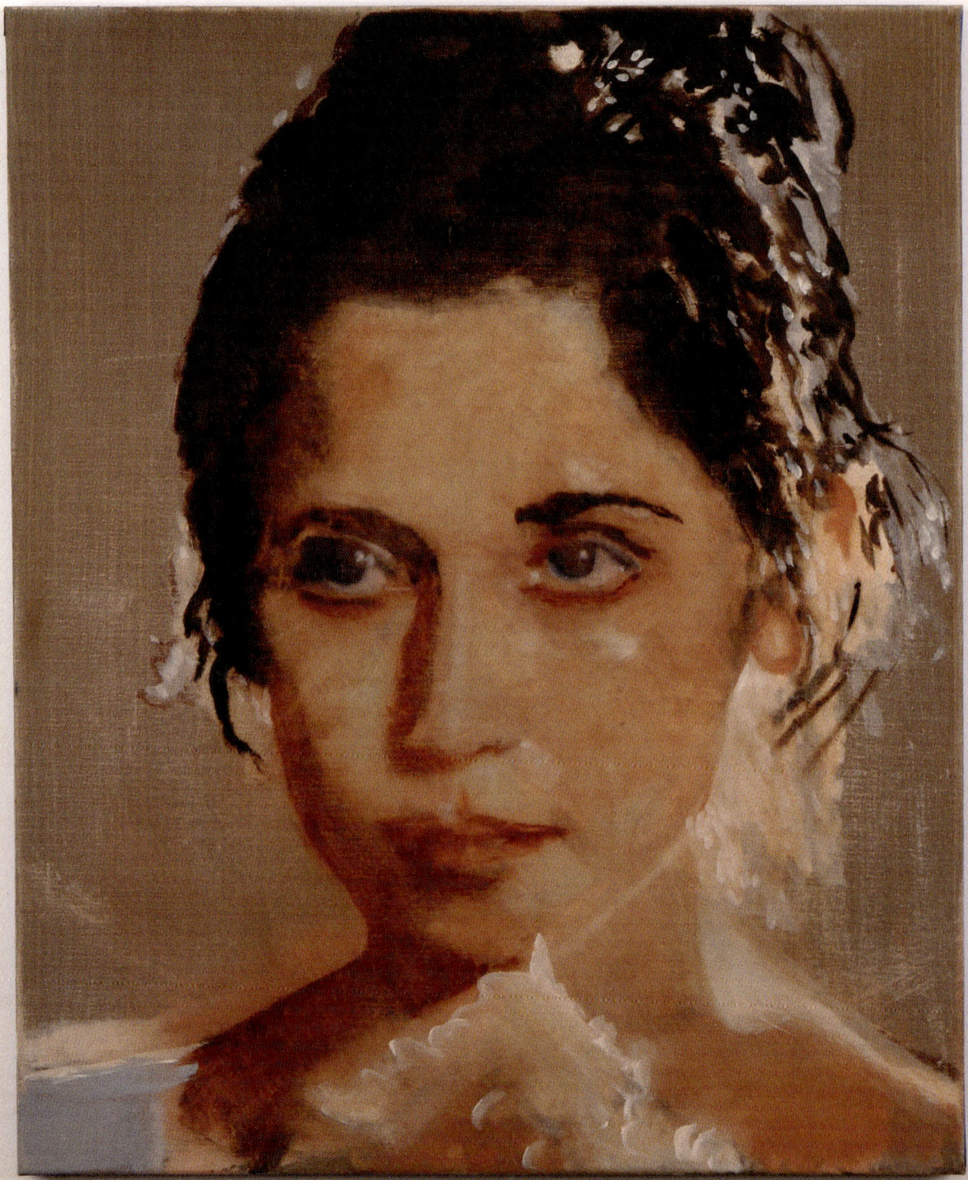

Nora Brady, the beautiful woman who caused Barry to become a wanderer, 2006
oil on linen, 76 x 61 cm
collection Van Dam, the Netherlands

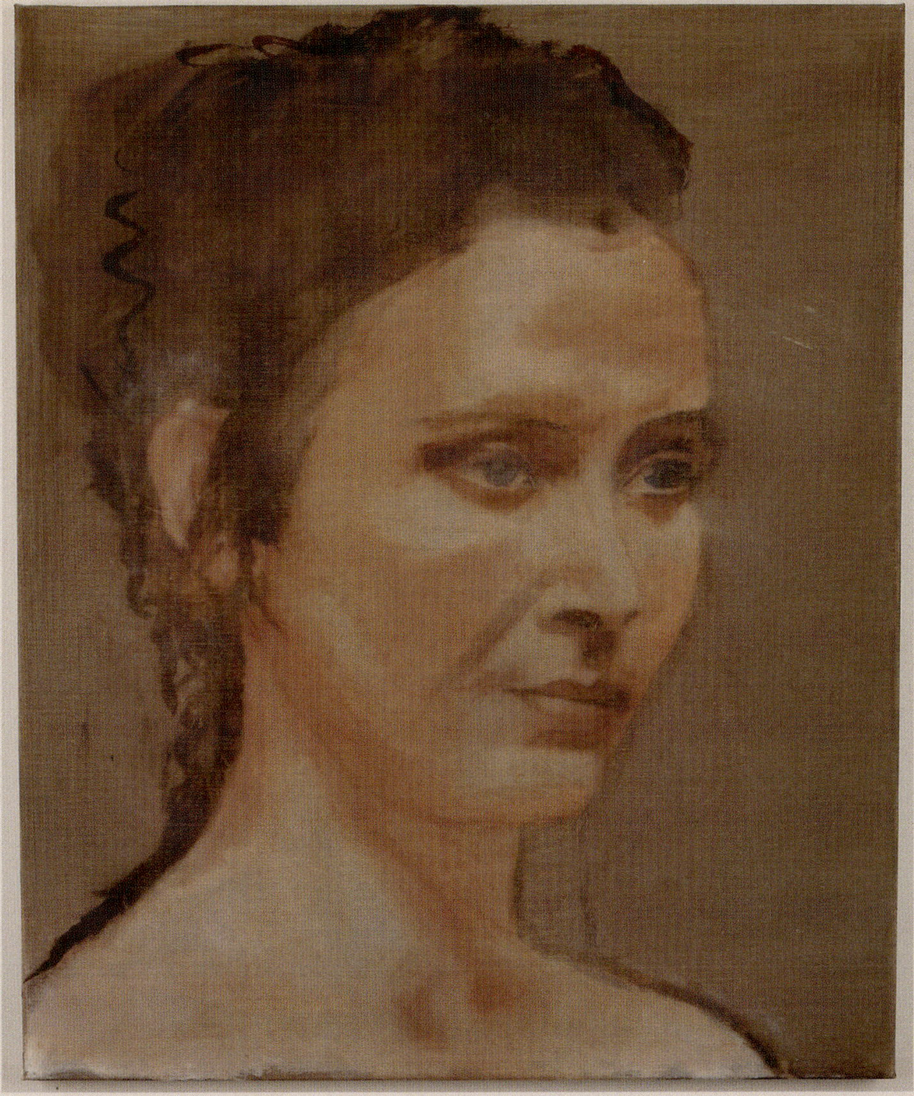

Nora Brady, 2006
oil on linen, 76 x 61 cm
private collection, the Netherlands

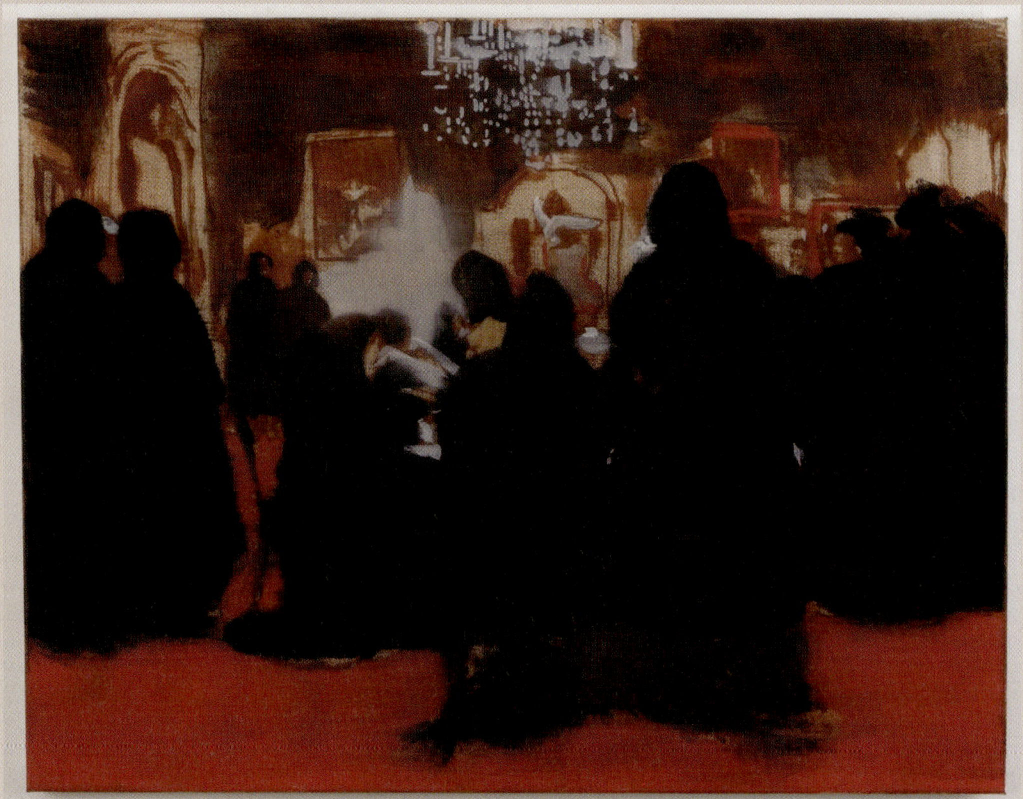

Sketch for Sex, 2006
oil on linen, 60 x 76 cm
private collection, USA

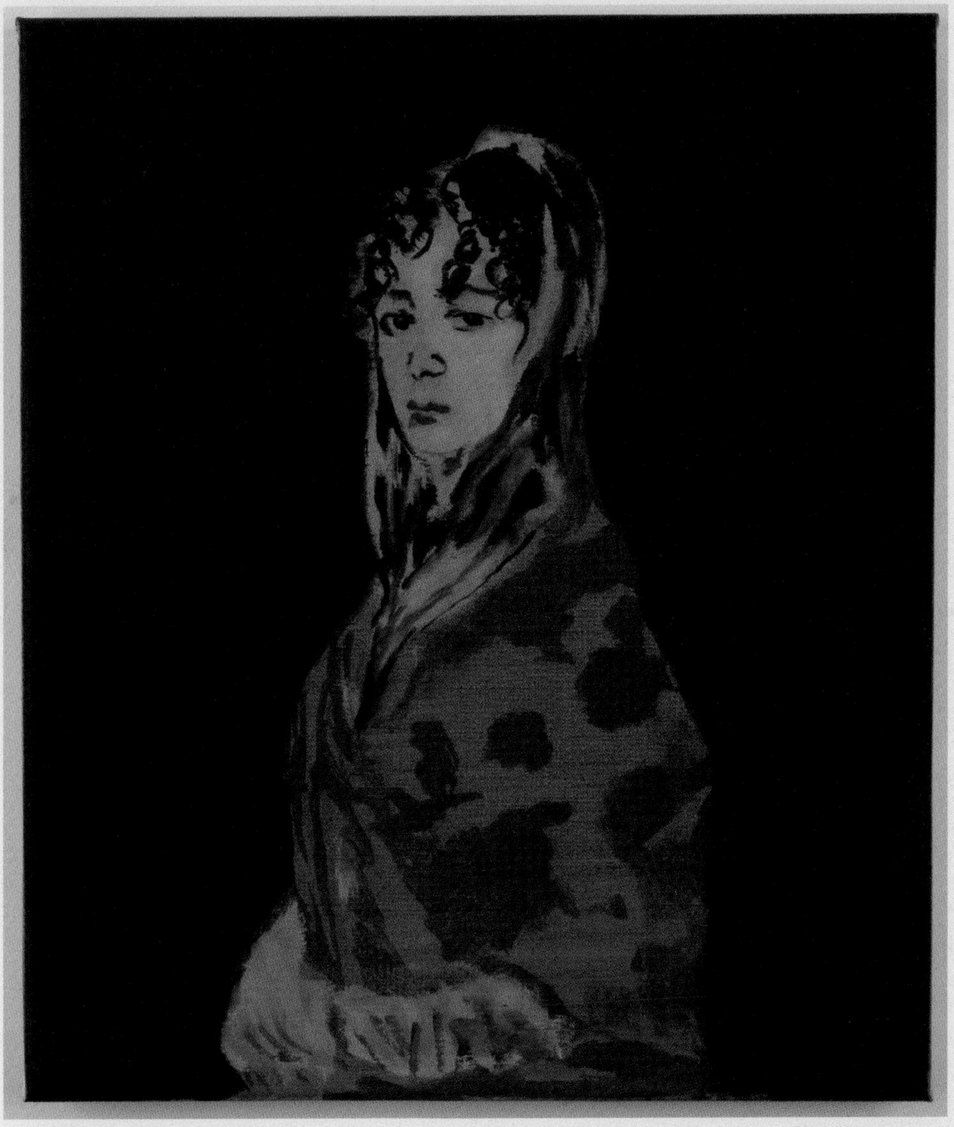

Francisca Sabasa y Garcia; the emancipation of women cautiously proceeding, 2007
oil on linen, 43 x 35,5 cm
collection Gauthier-Symersky, the Netherlands

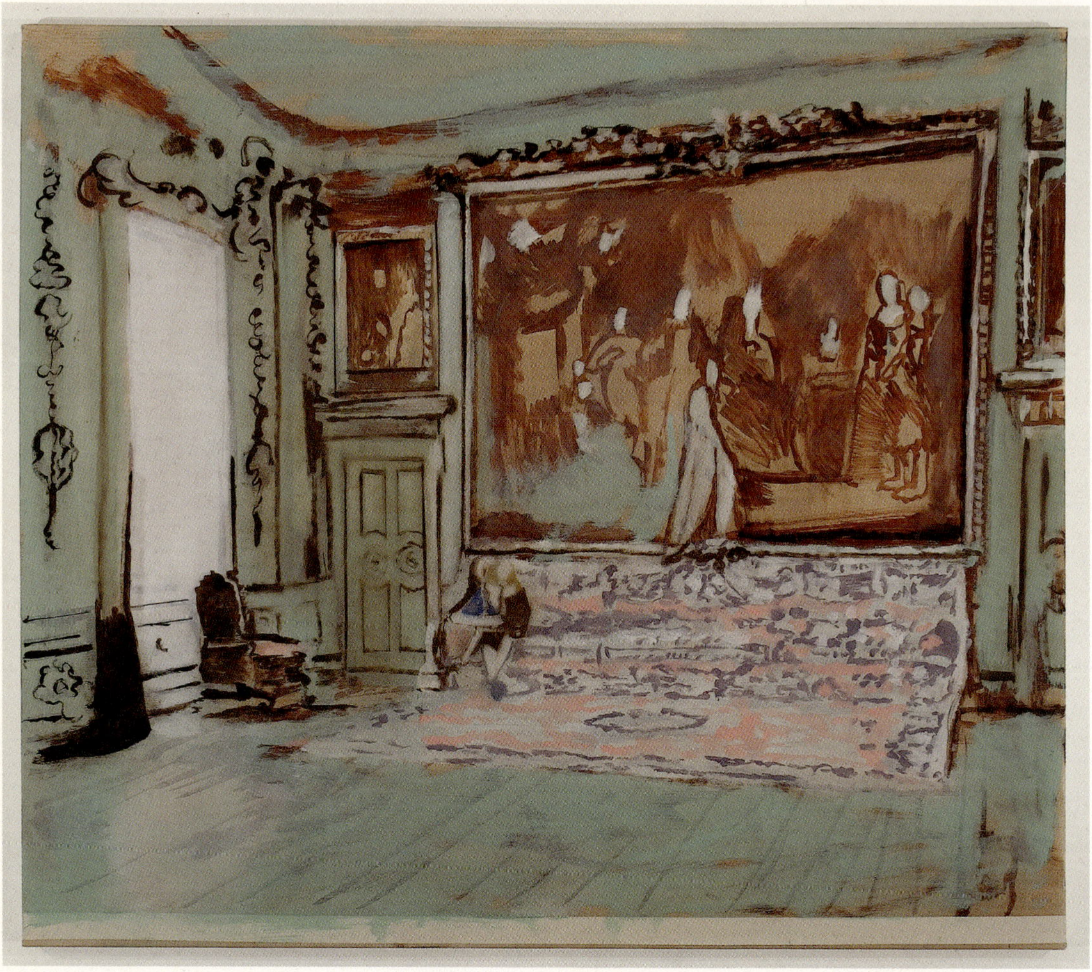

Family, 2007
oil on linen, 151 x 200 cm
courtesy Galerie Tanya Rumpff, Haarlem, the Netherlands

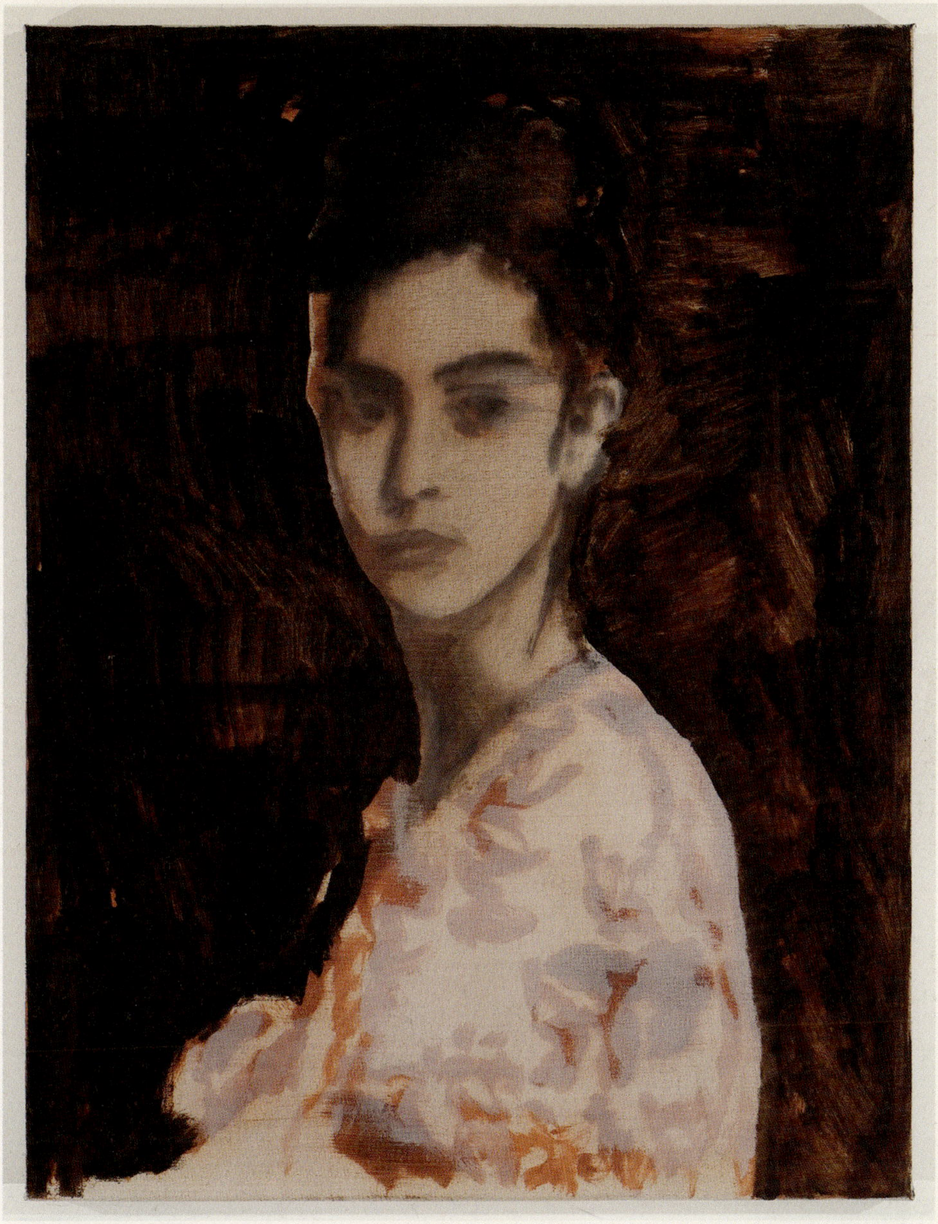

Salome, 2007
oil on linen, 60 x 45 cm
courtesy Galerie Tanya Rumpff, Haarlem, the Netherlands

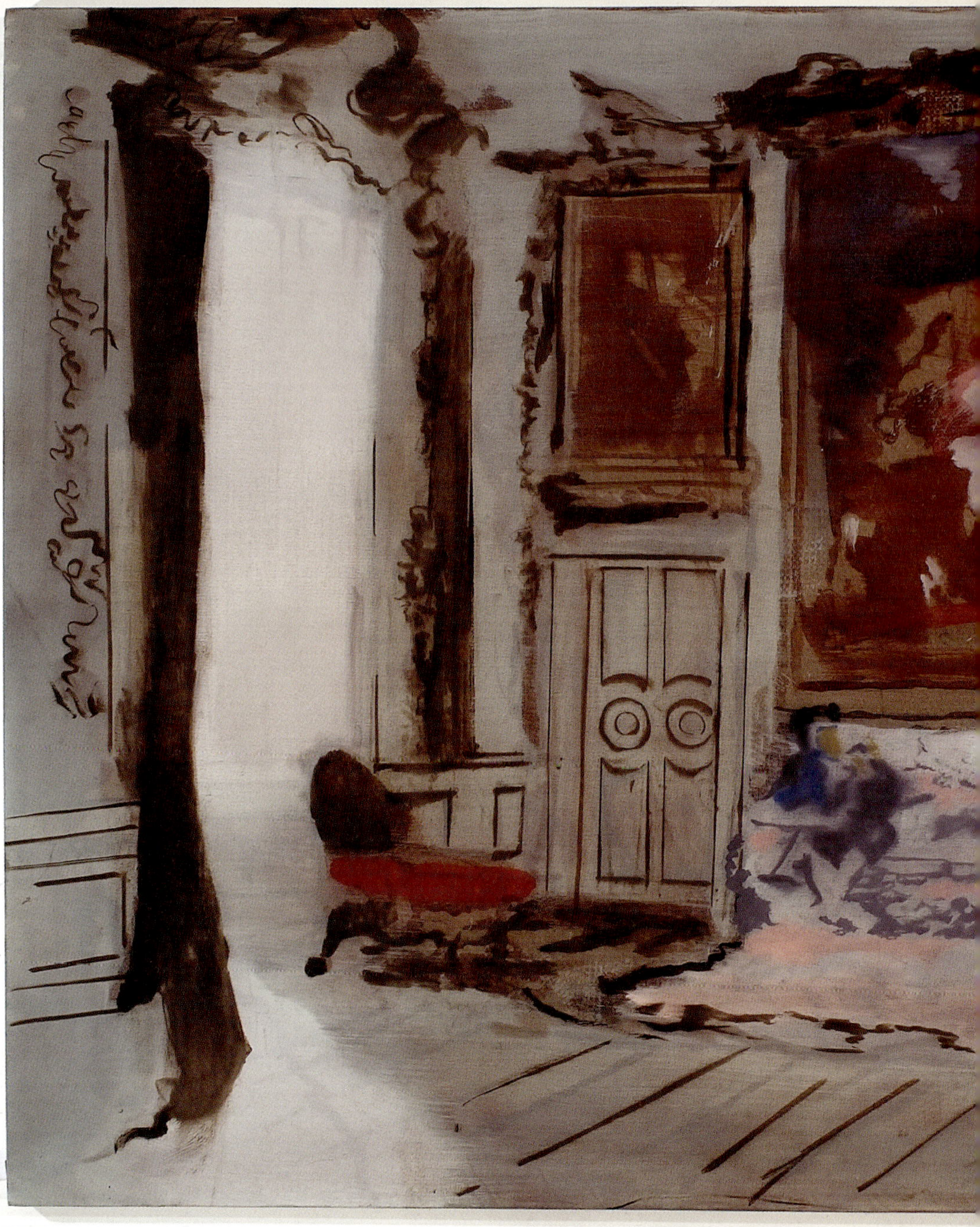

Family, 2006
oil on linen, 134 x 200 cm
courtesy Artcore/Fabrice Marcolini, Toronto, Canada

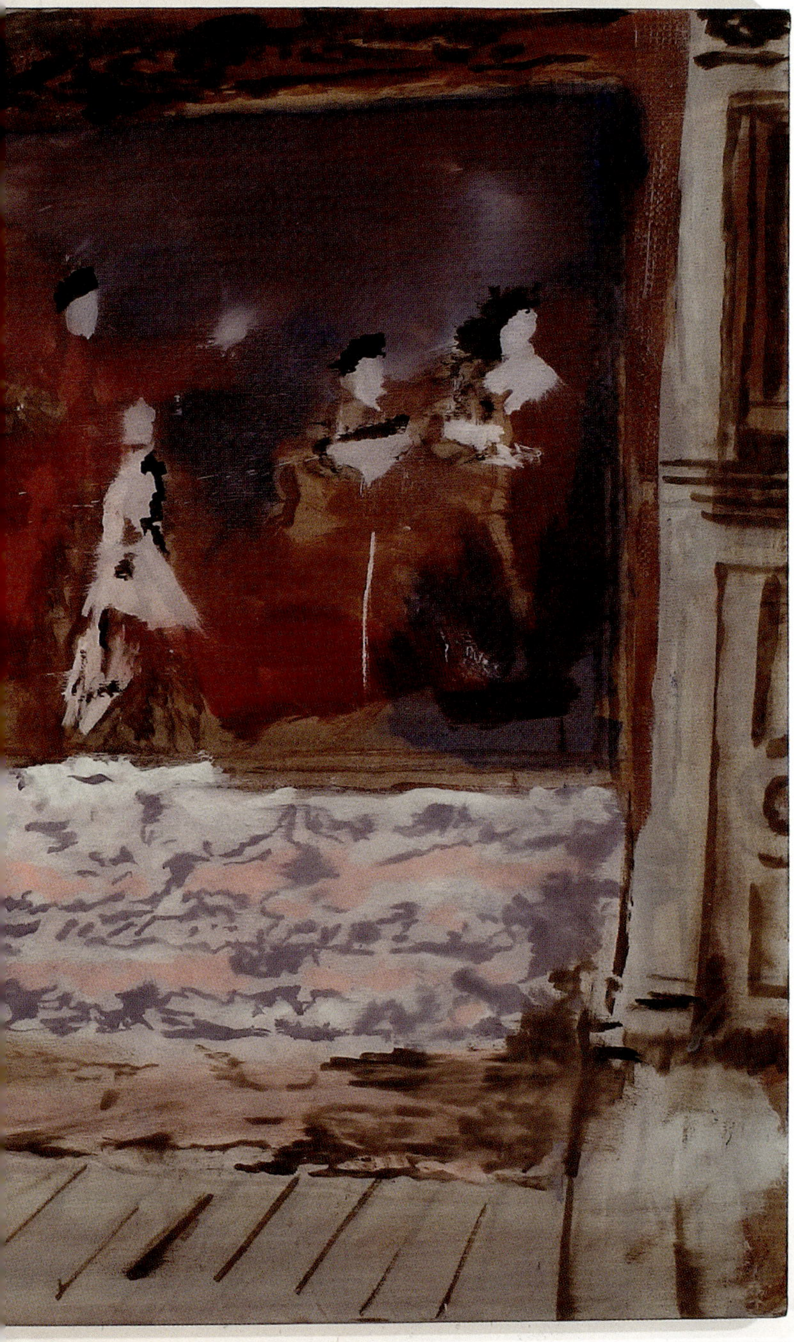

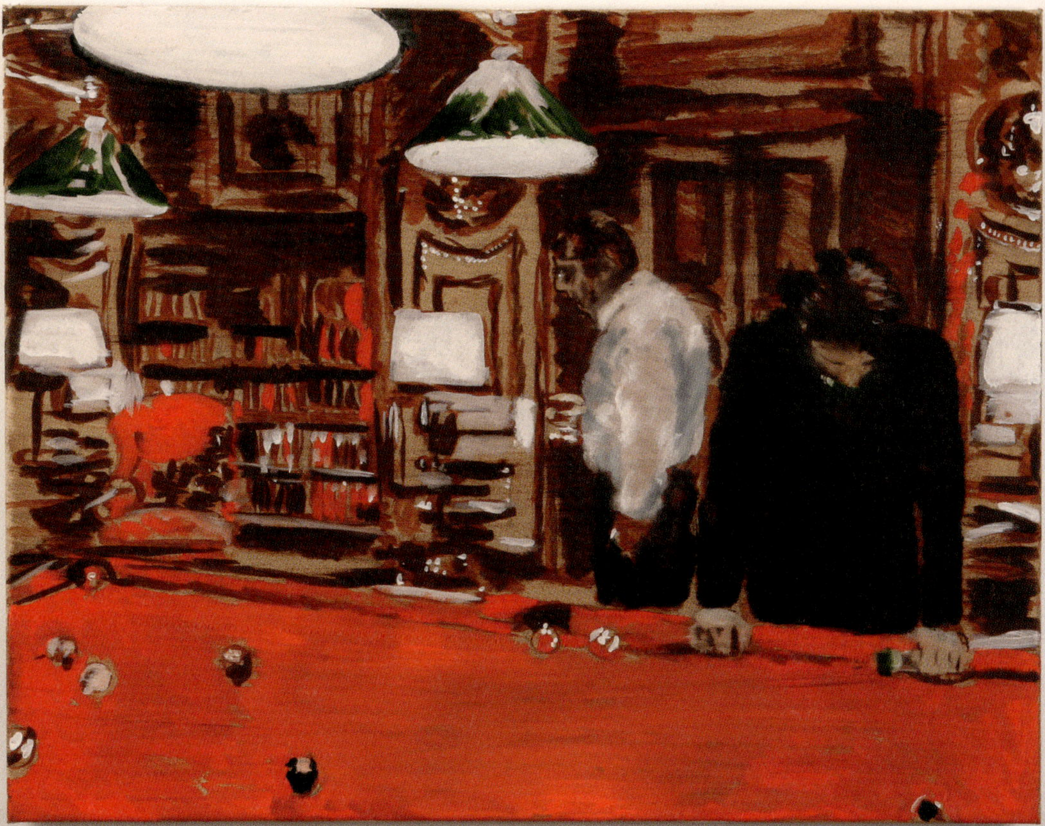

Sketch for Family, 2006
oil on linen, 60 x 76 cm
courtesy Torch Gallery, Amsterdam, the Netherlands

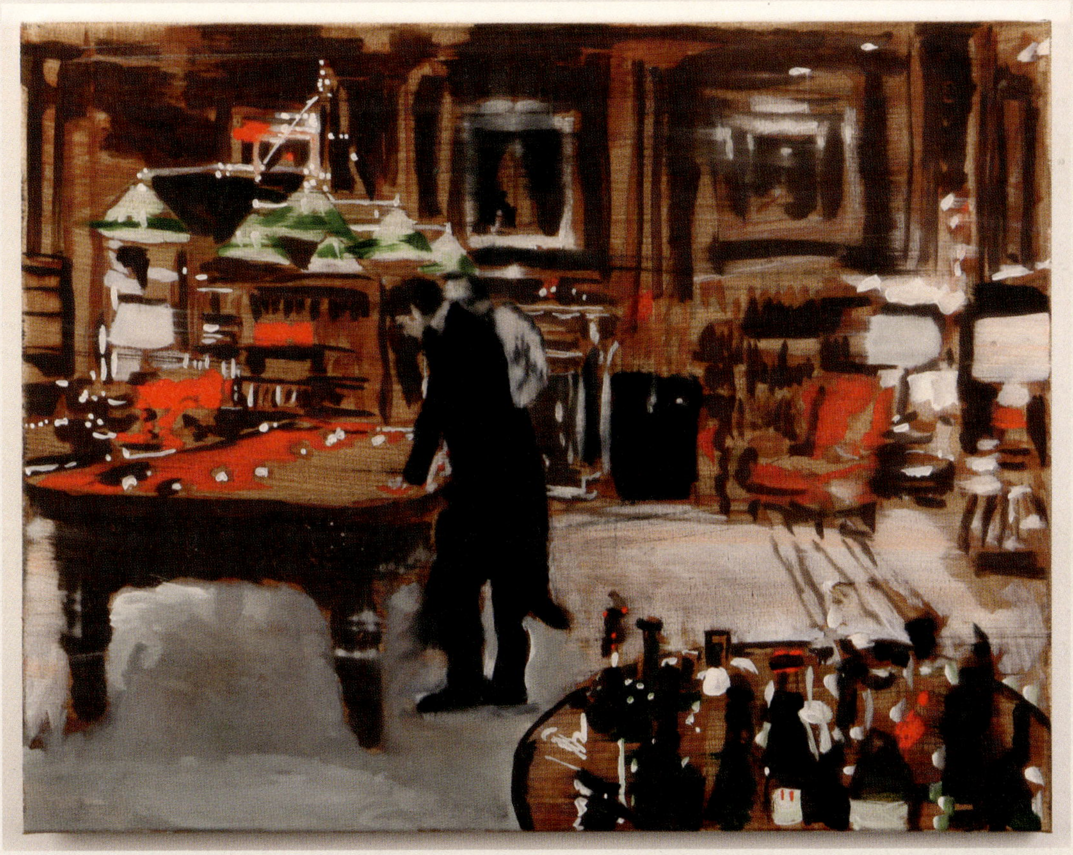

Sketch for Family, 2006
oil on linen, 60 x 76 cm
courtesy Torch Gallery, Amsterdam, the Netherlands

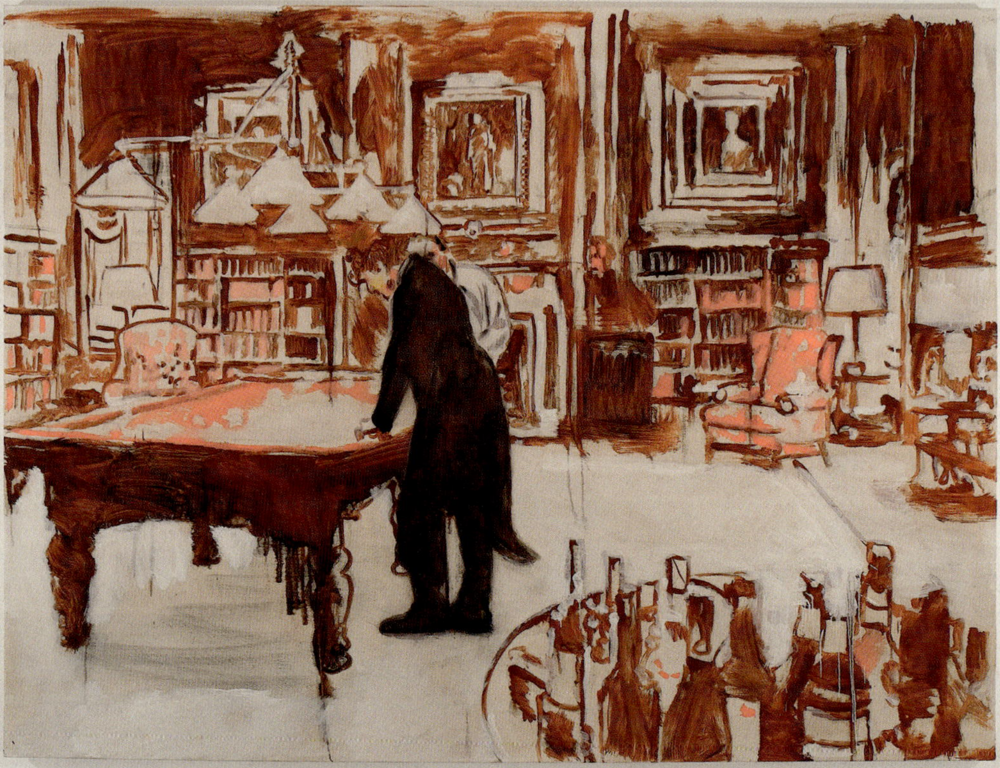

Conversation, 2007
oil on linen, 155 x 200 cm
courtesy Galerie Fahnemann, Berlin, Germany

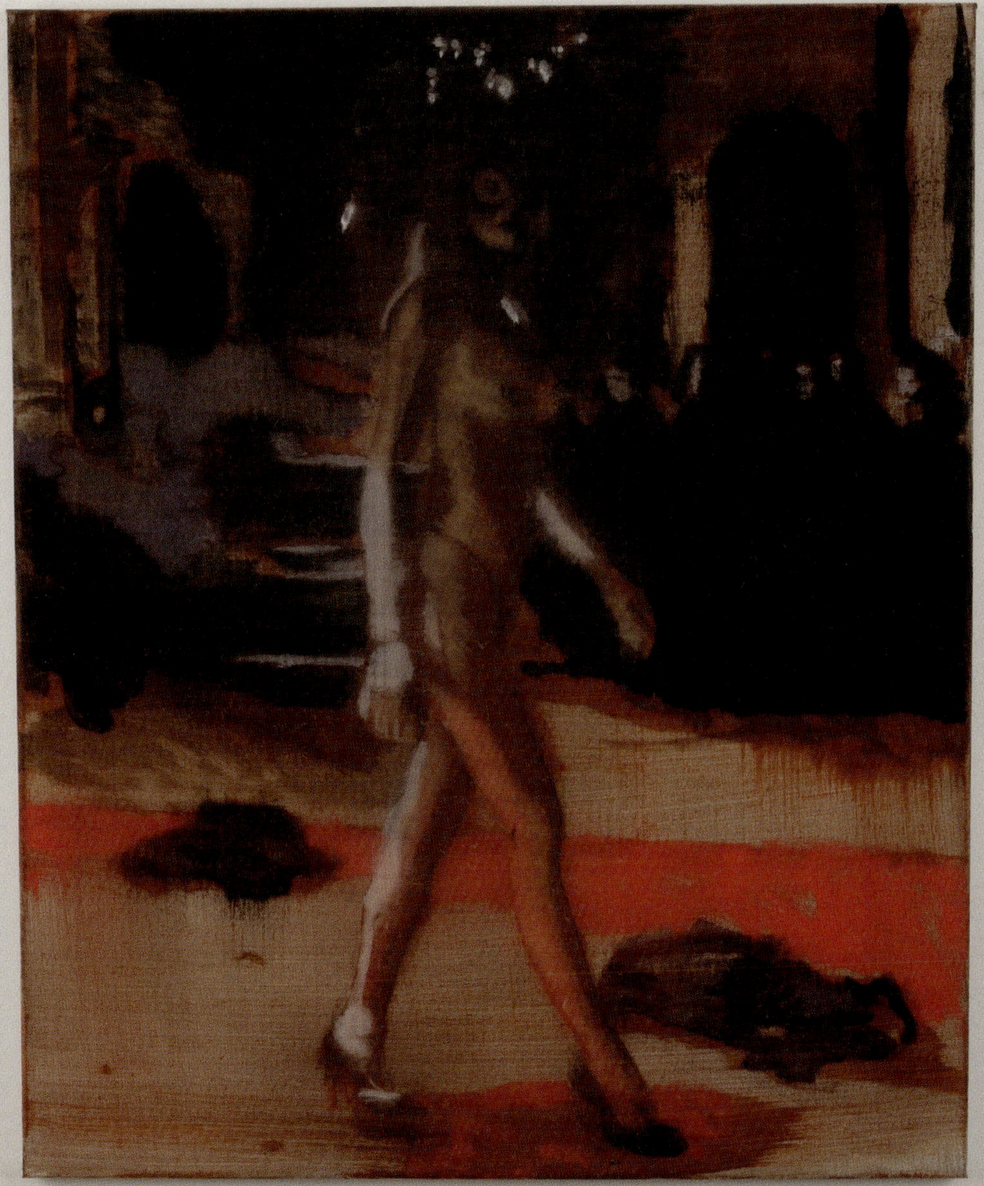

Sketch for Reality, 2006
oil on linen, 76 x 60 cm
courtesy Artcore/Fabrice Marcolini, Toronto, Canada

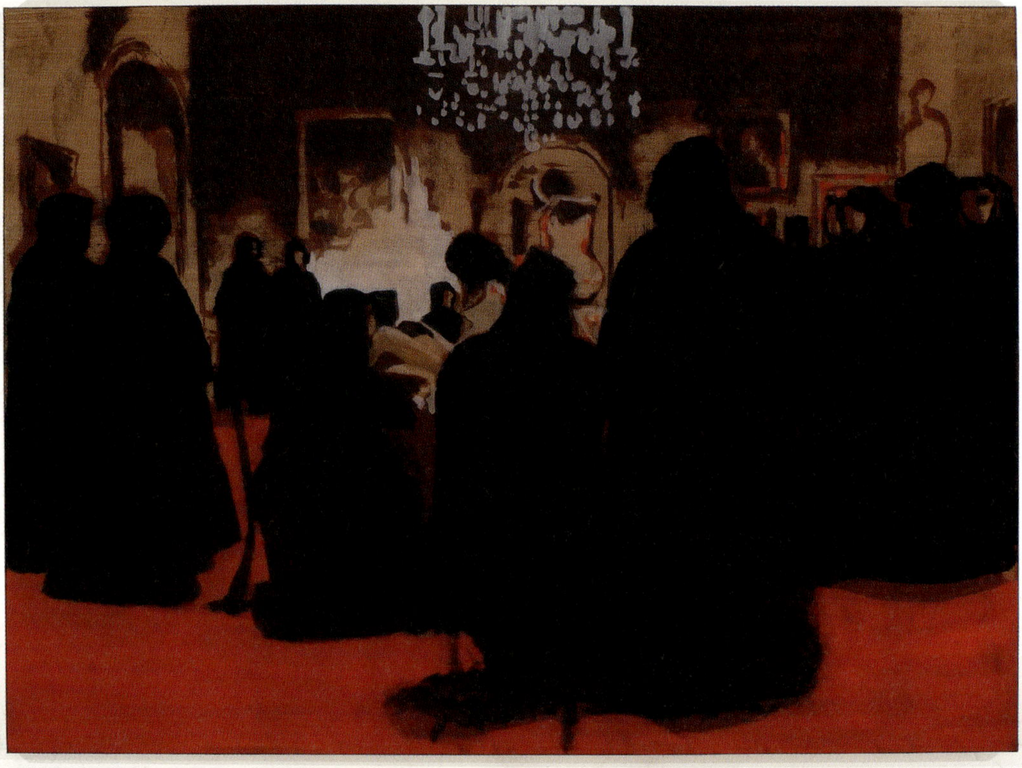

Sex, 2006
oil on linen, 150 x 200 cm
Private collection, Toronto, Canada

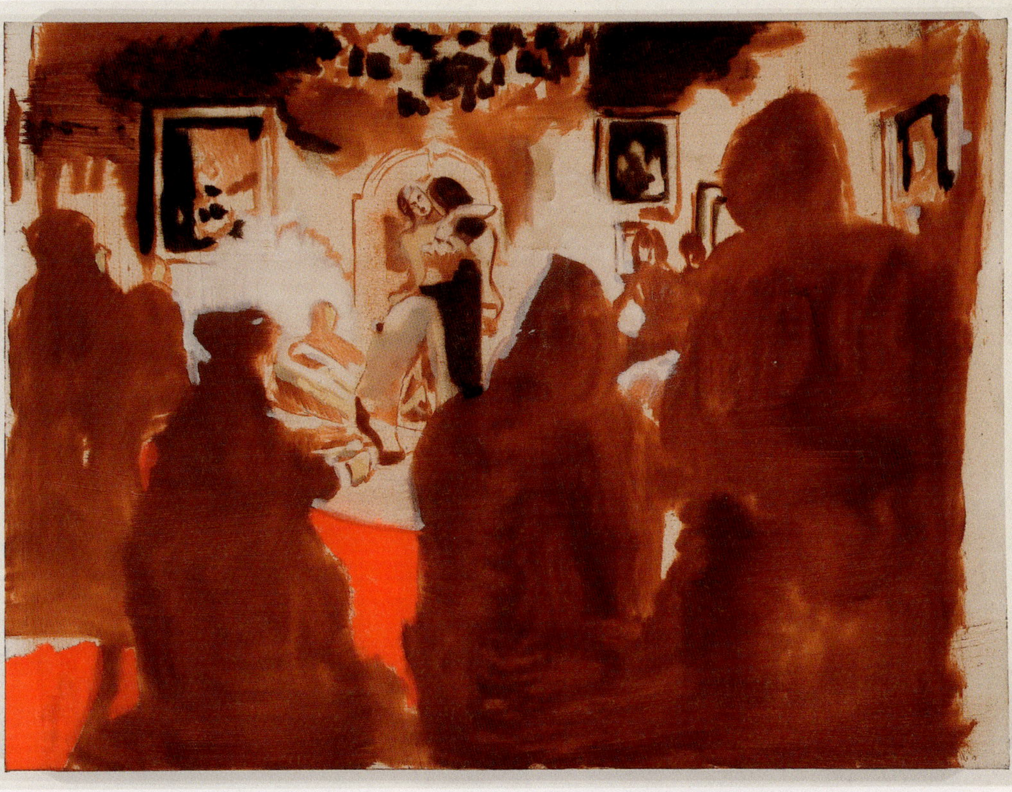

Sex, 2007
oil on linen, 91 x 122 cm
courtesy Galerie Tanya Rumpff, Haarlem, the Netherlands

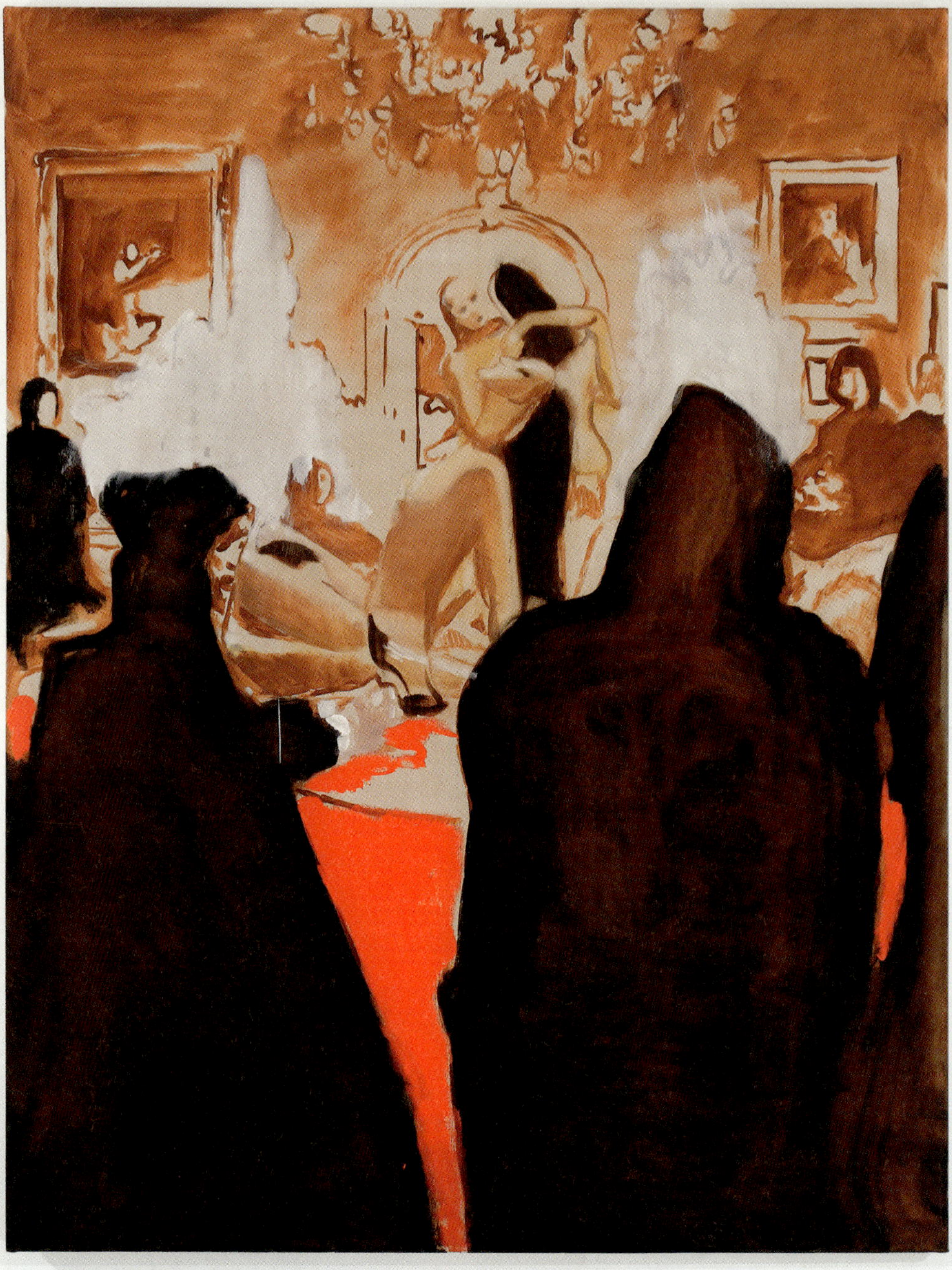

Sex, 2007
oil on linen, 200 x 150 cm
courtesy Newman Popiashvili Gallery, New York

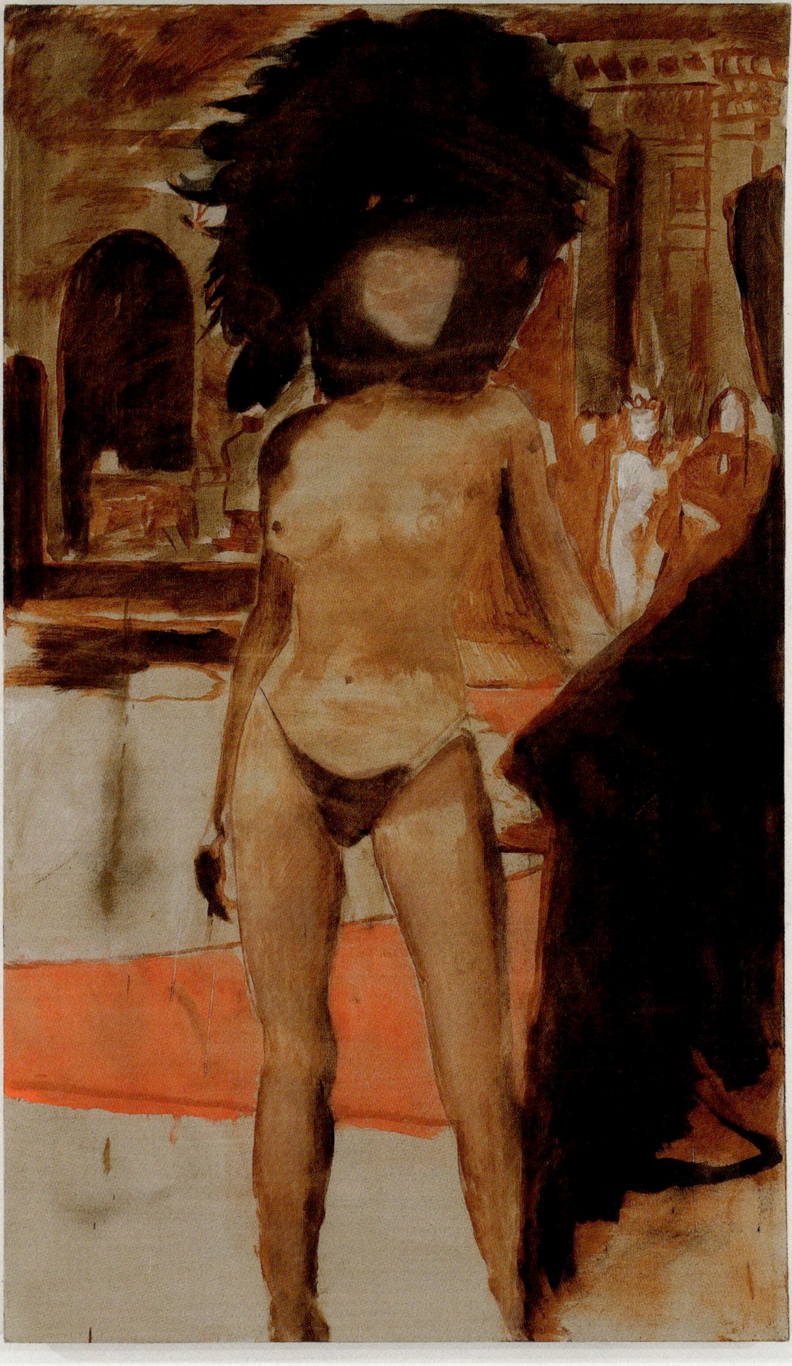

Hooker, 2007
oil on linen, 200,5 x 115 cm
courtesy Newman Popiashvili Gallery, New York

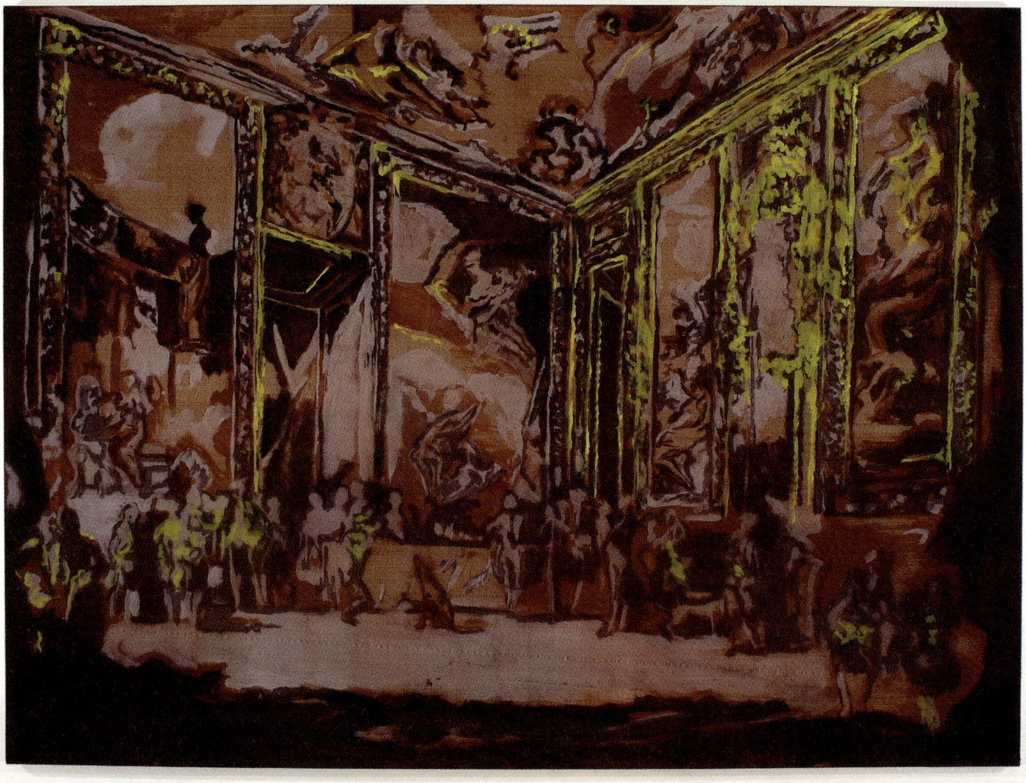

Lunch, 2006
oil on linen, 155 x 201 cm
courtesy Torch Gallery, Amsterdam, the Netherlands

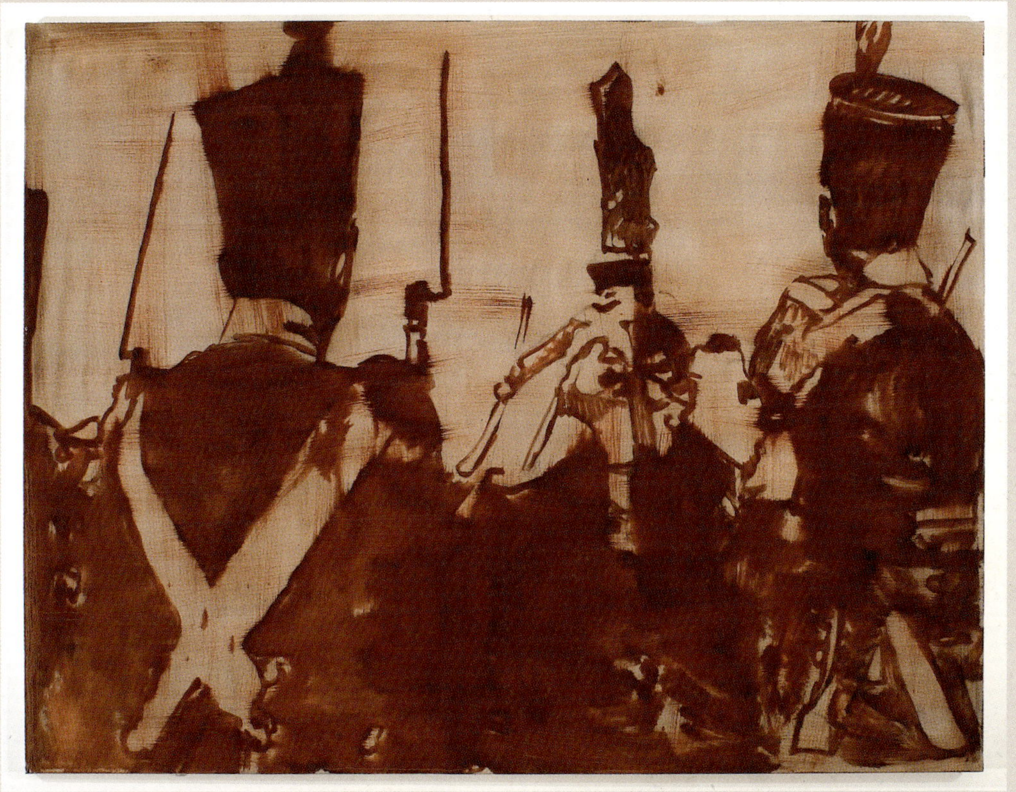

Execution, 2006
oil on linen, 157 x 200 cm
courtesy Artcore/Fabrice Marcolini, Toronto, Canada

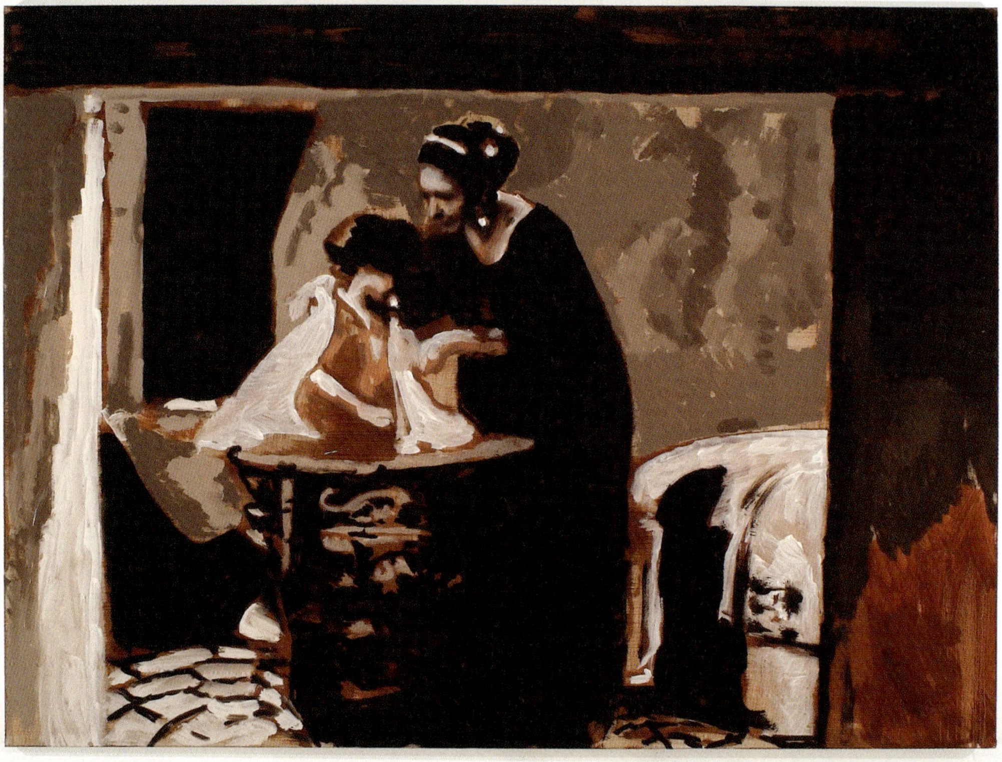

Medea, 2006
oil on linen, 150 x 200 cm
courtesy Artcore/Fabrice Marcolini, Toronto, Canada

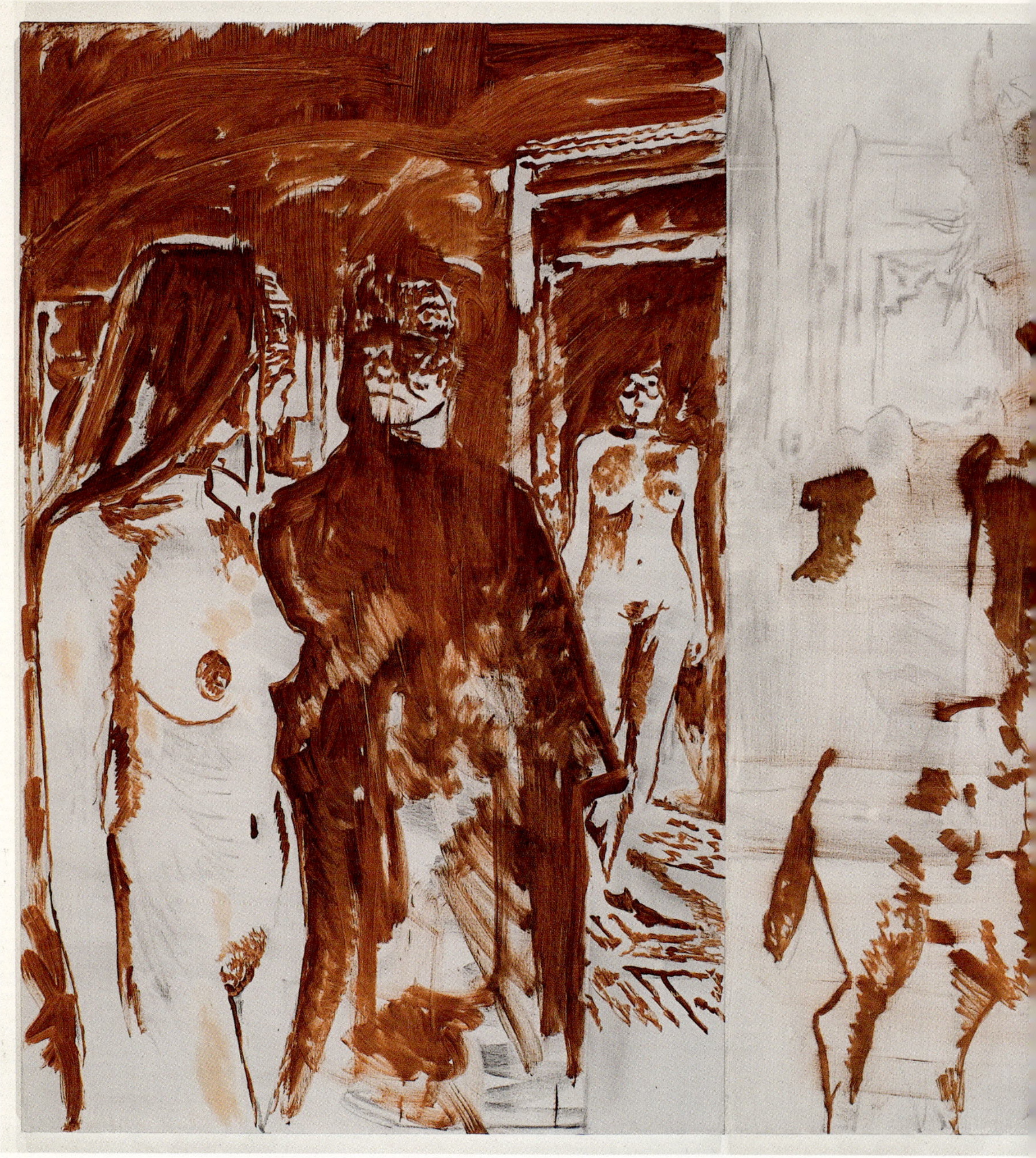

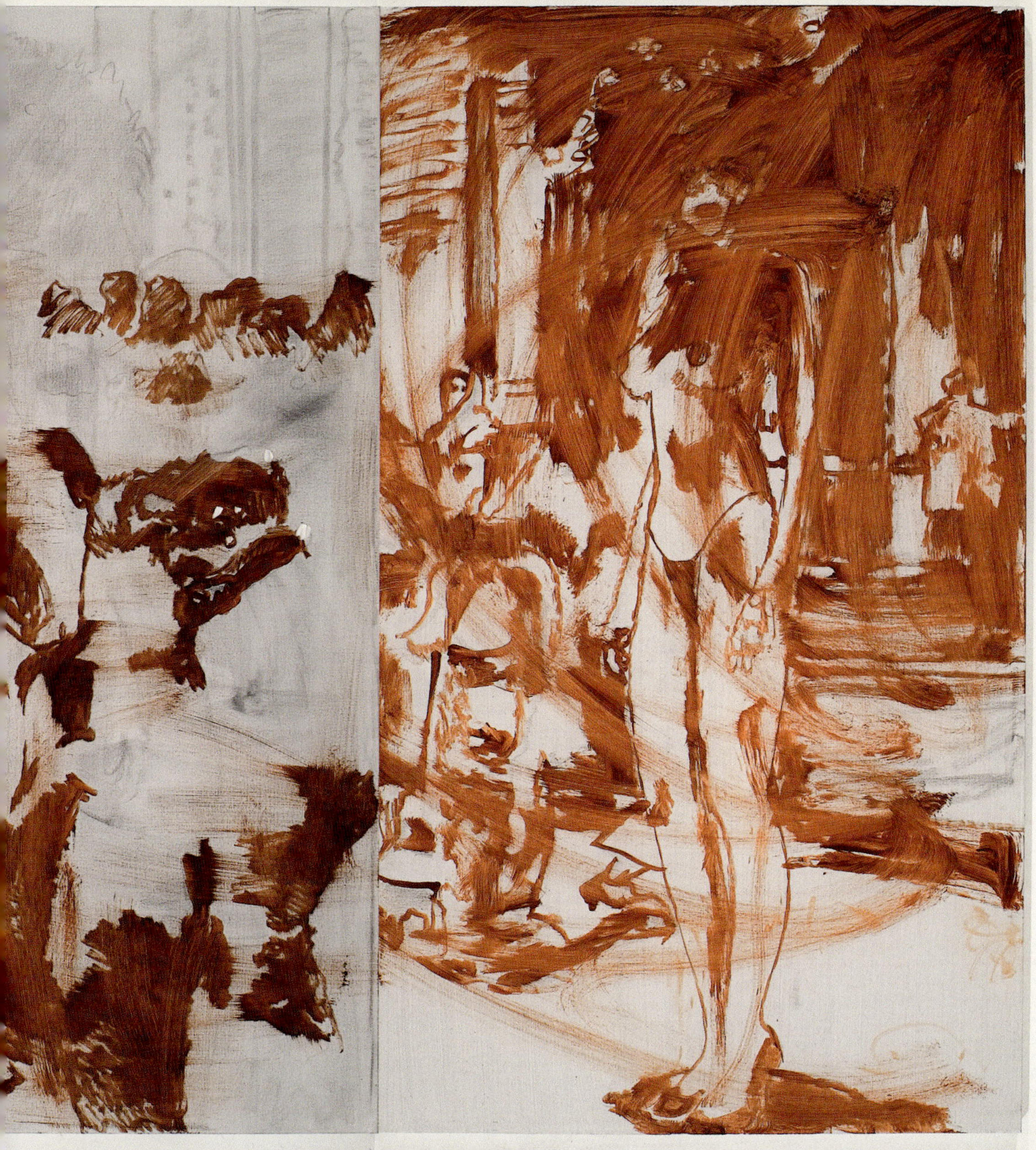

Politics, 2007
oil on linen, 200 x 380 cm
courtesy Artcore/Fabrice Marcolini, Toronto, Canada

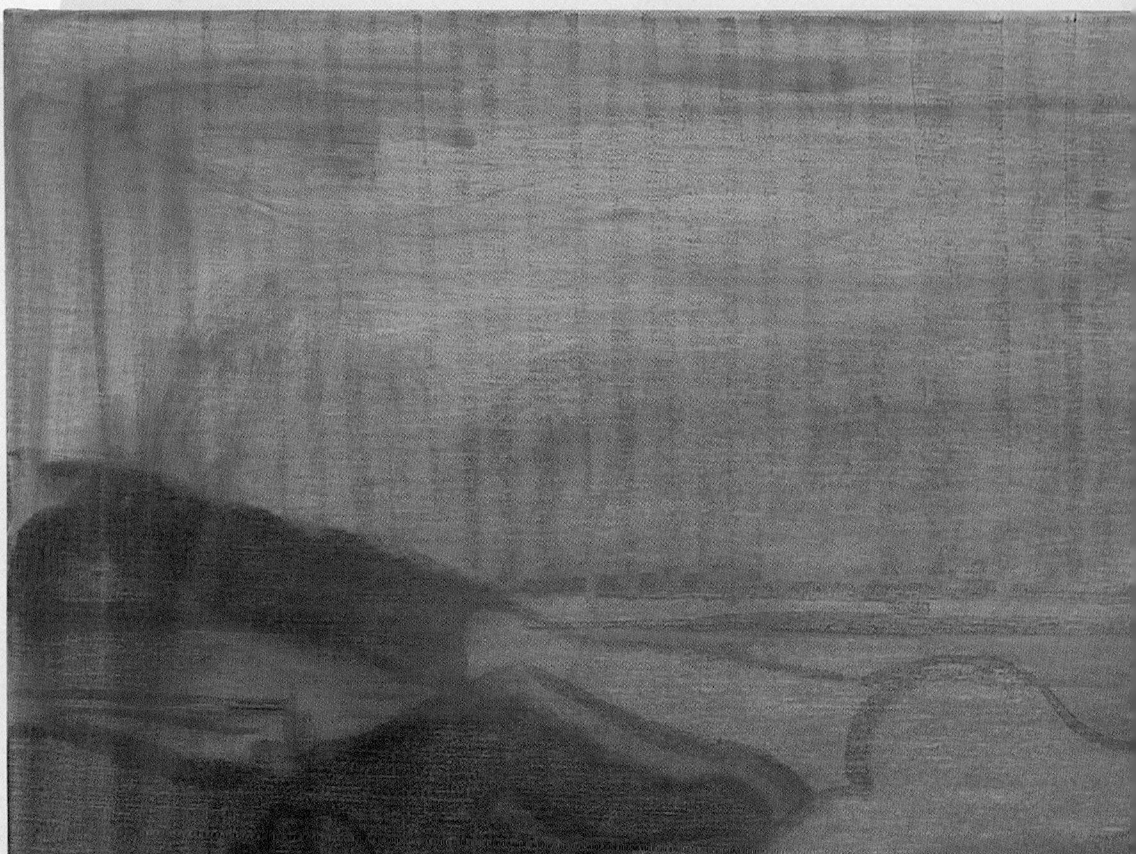

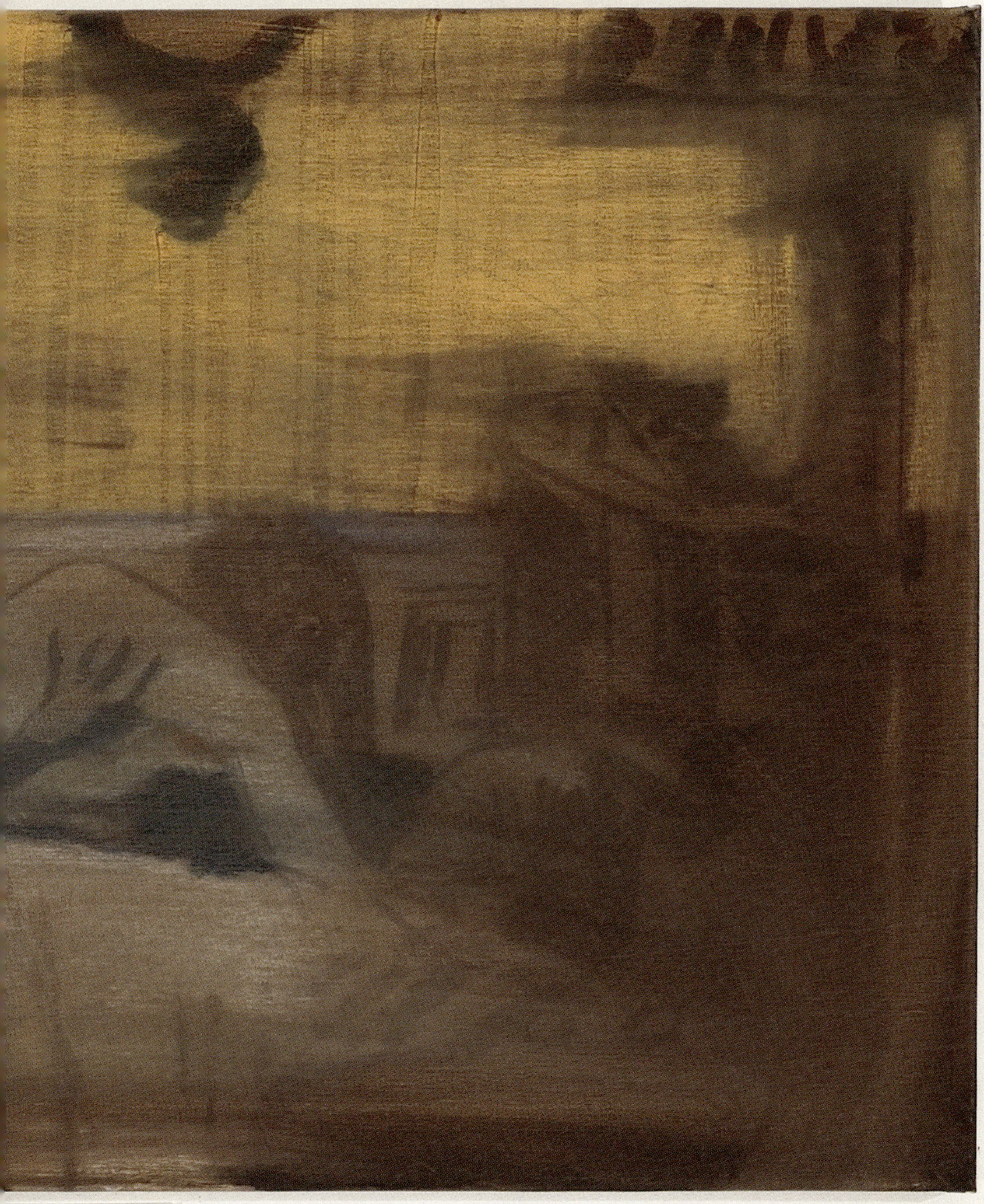

Gold, 2006
oil on linen, 56 x 96 cm
courtesy Artcore/Fabrice Marcolini, Toronto, Canada

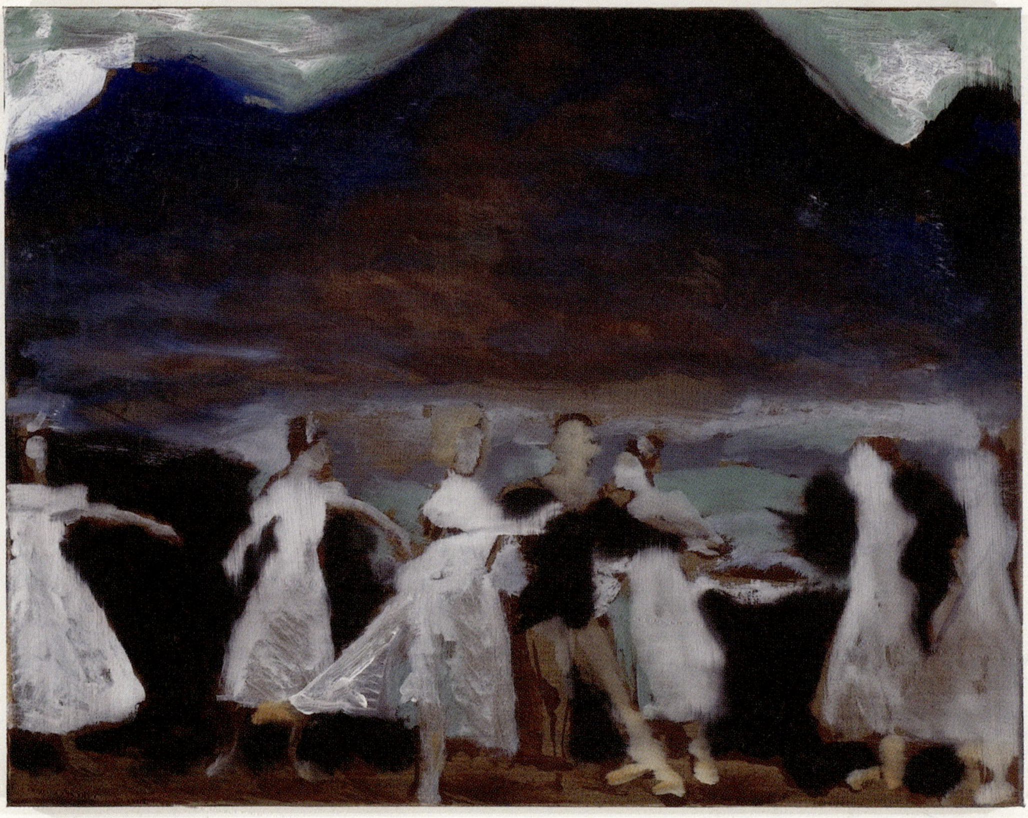

Sketch for Dans, 2006
oil on linen, 61 x 76 cm
courtesy Artcore/Fabrice Marcolini, Toronto, Canada

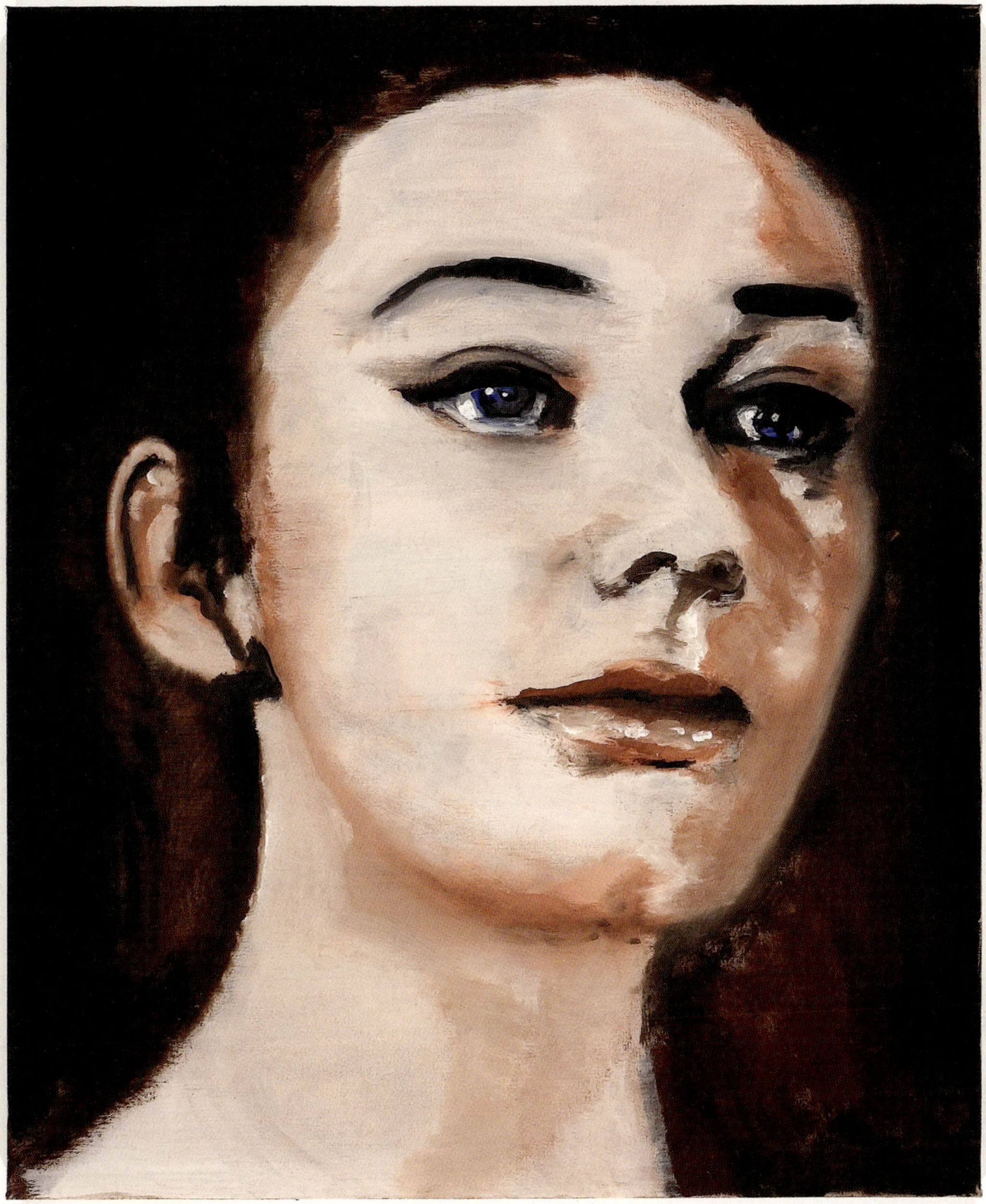

Natasha Rostova (unusually charming due to her exuberant, enthusiastic personality), 2006
oil on linen, 61 x 76 cm
collection Eric Decelle, Bruxelles, Belgium

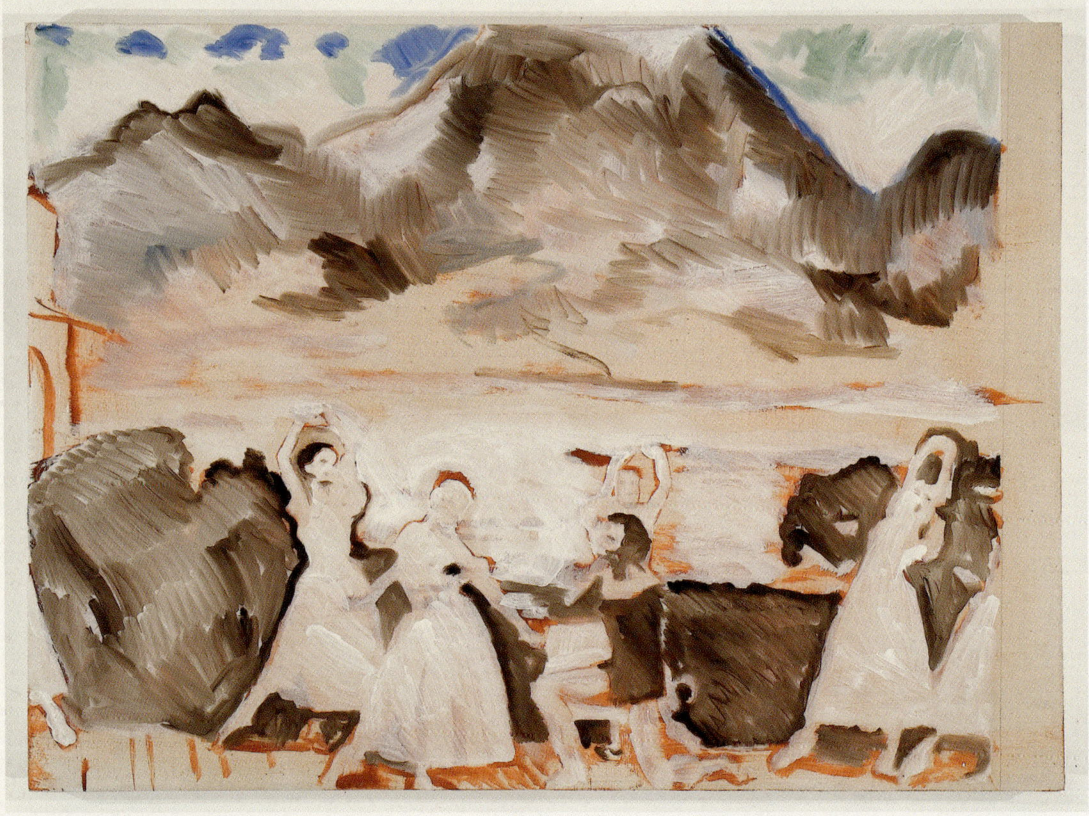

Dance, 2007
oil on linen, 91 x 113 cm
courtesy Galerie Tanya Rumpff, Haarlem, the Netherlands

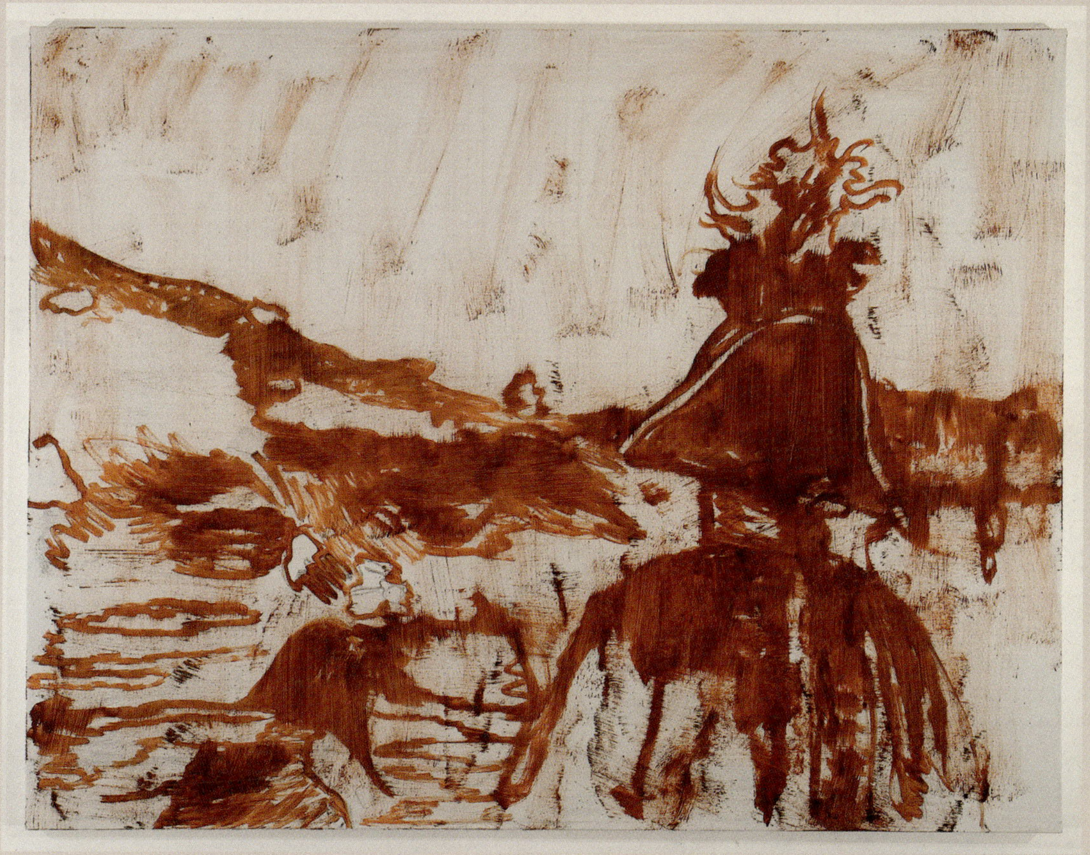

Officers, 2007
oil on linen, 157 x 200 cm
collection Eric Decelle, Bruxelles, Belgium

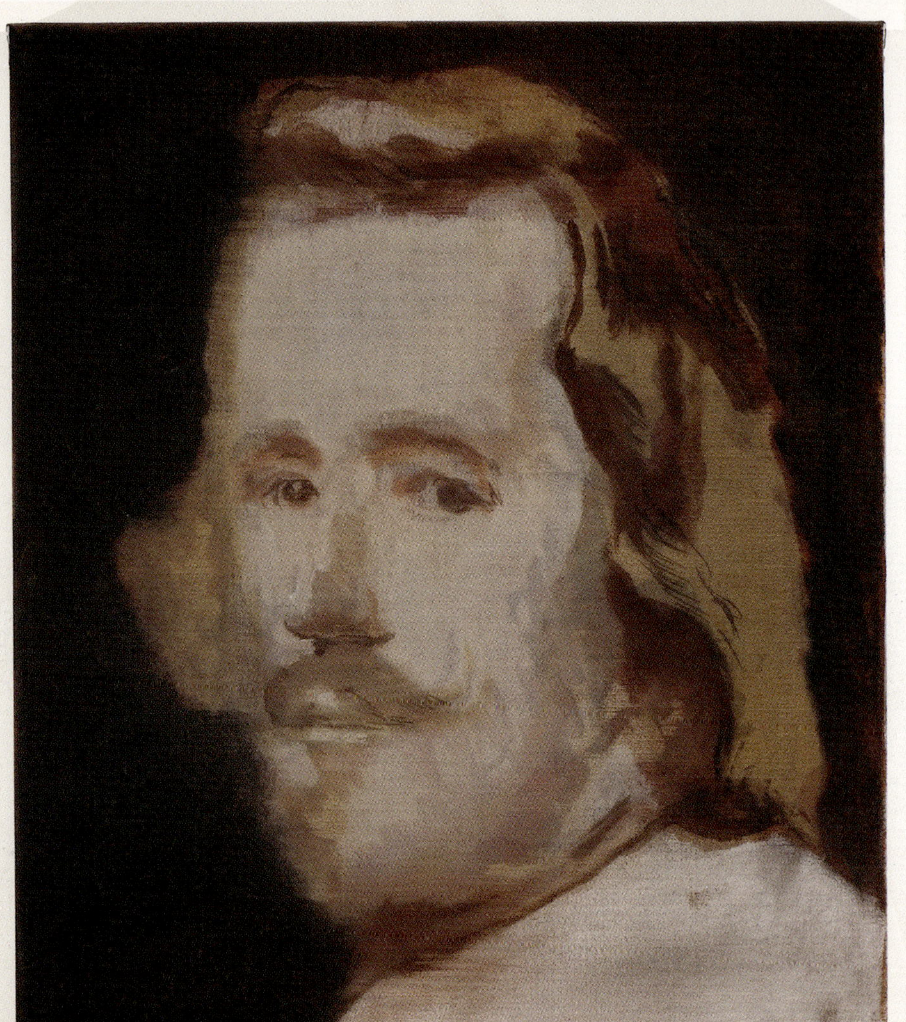

Felipe Cuarto, 2006
oil on linen, 43 x 35,5 cm
courtesy Galerie Fahnemann, Berlin, Germany

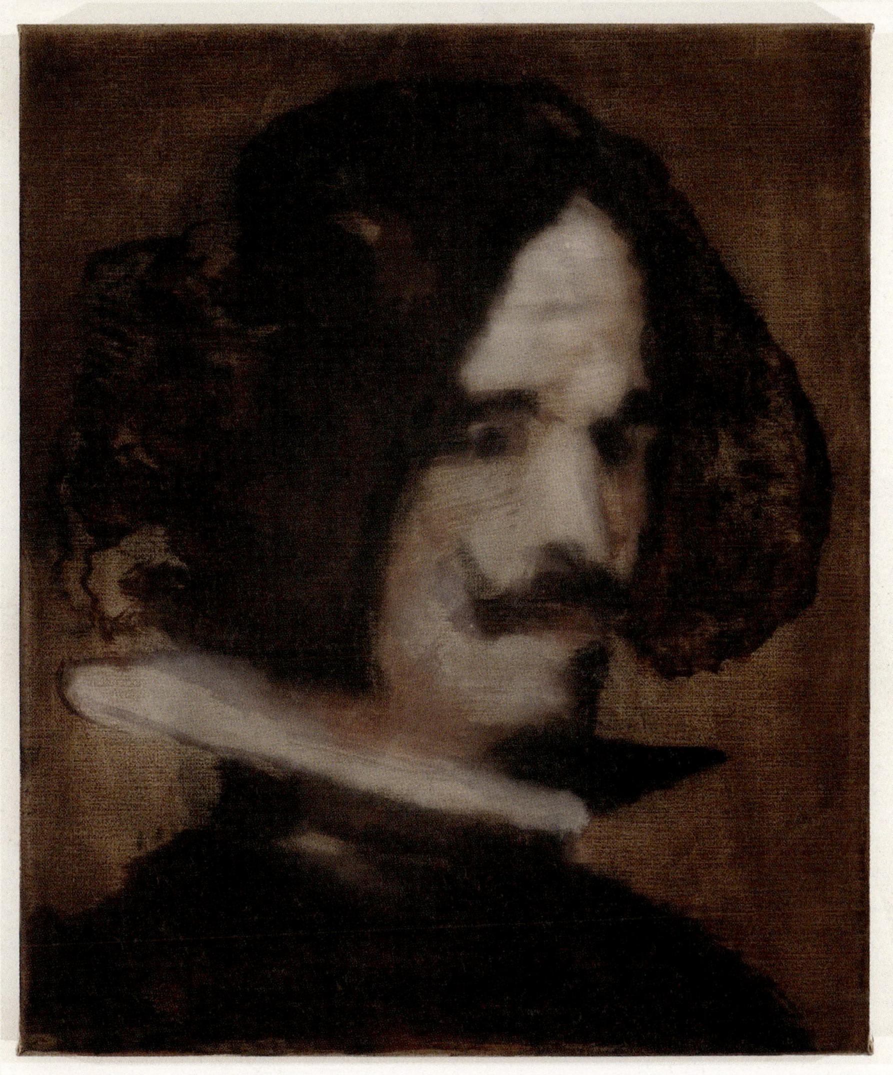

Velasquez, 2006
oil on linen, 43 x 35,5 cm
Collection of Paul Sorbara, Toronto, Canada

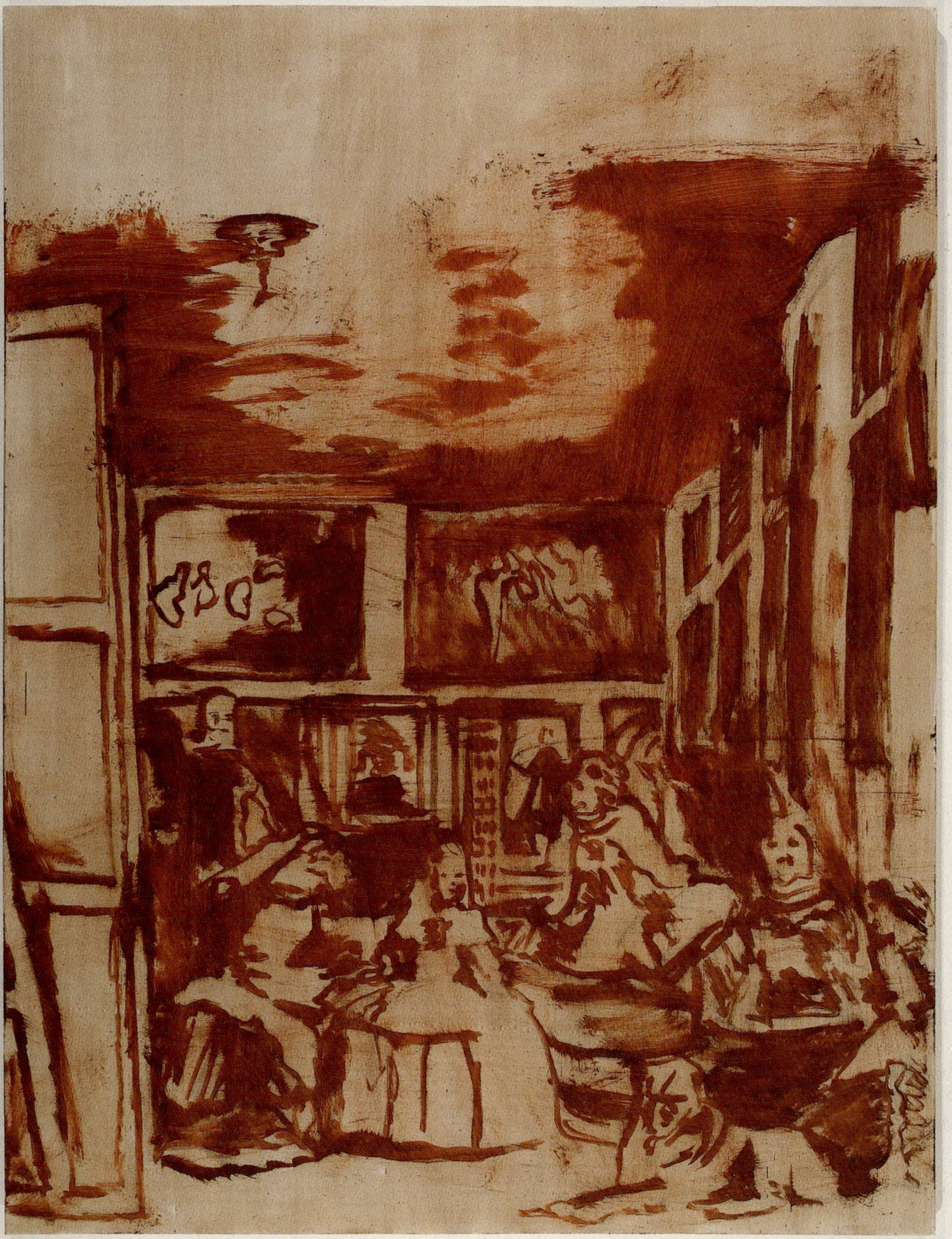

Family, 2007
oil on linen, 200 x 151 cm
courtesy Galerie Fahnemann, Berlin, Germany

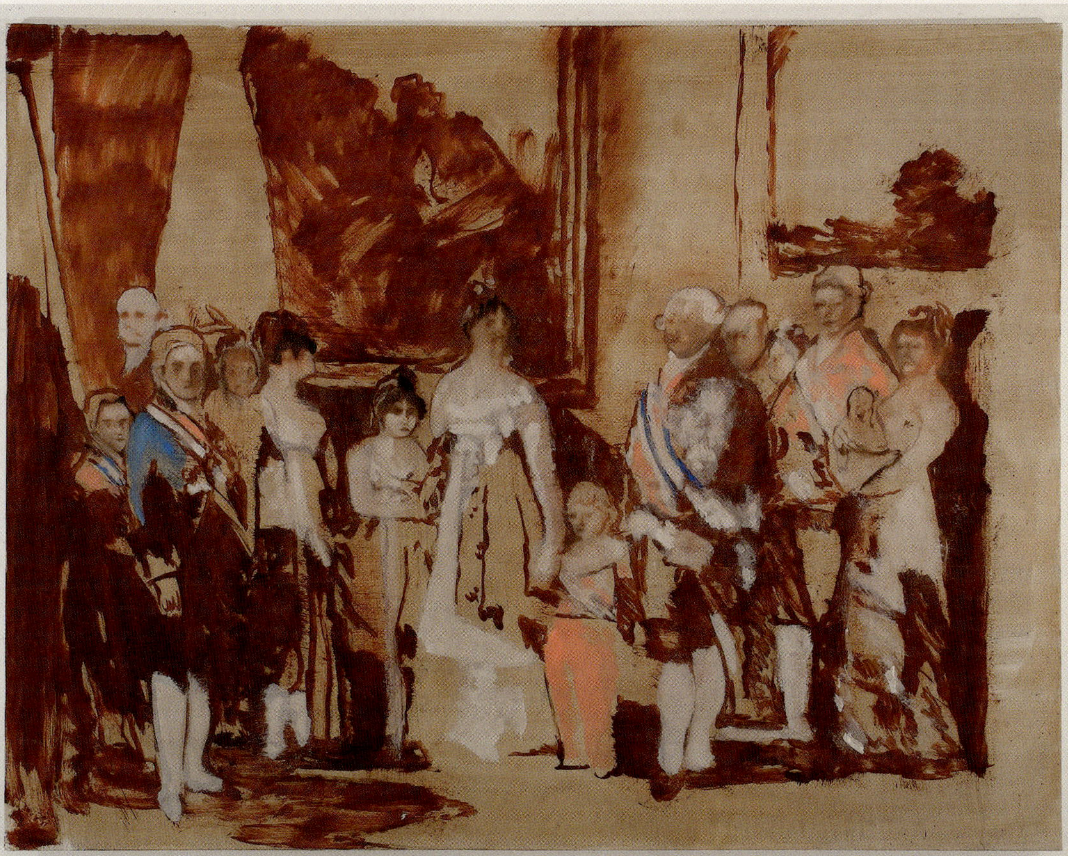

Family (unfinished), 2007
oil on linen, 160 x 200 cm
collection Eric Decelle, Bruxelles, Belgium

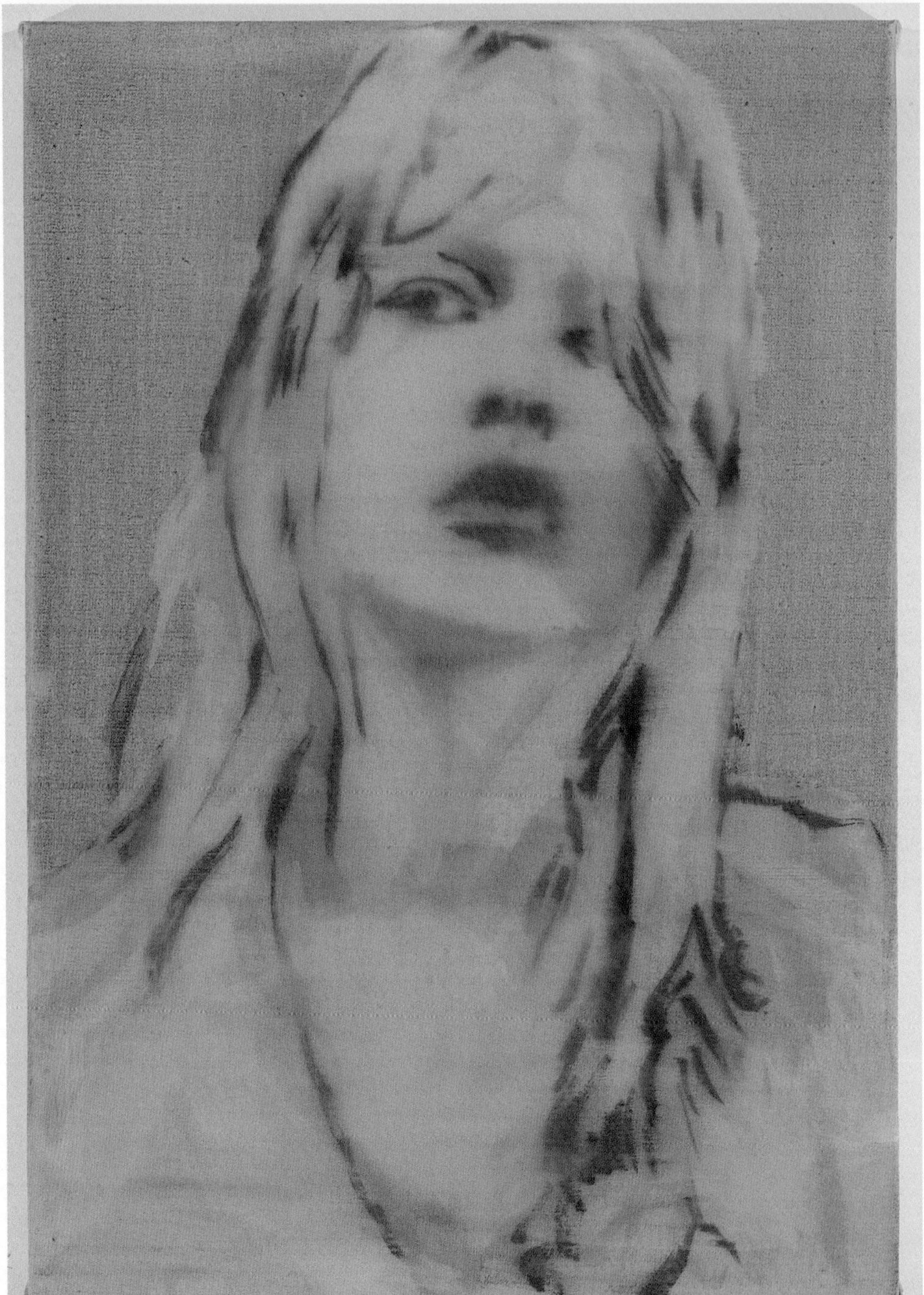

Polish model, 2007
oil on linen, 60,5 x 40,5 cm
collection Groenenboom, the Netherlands

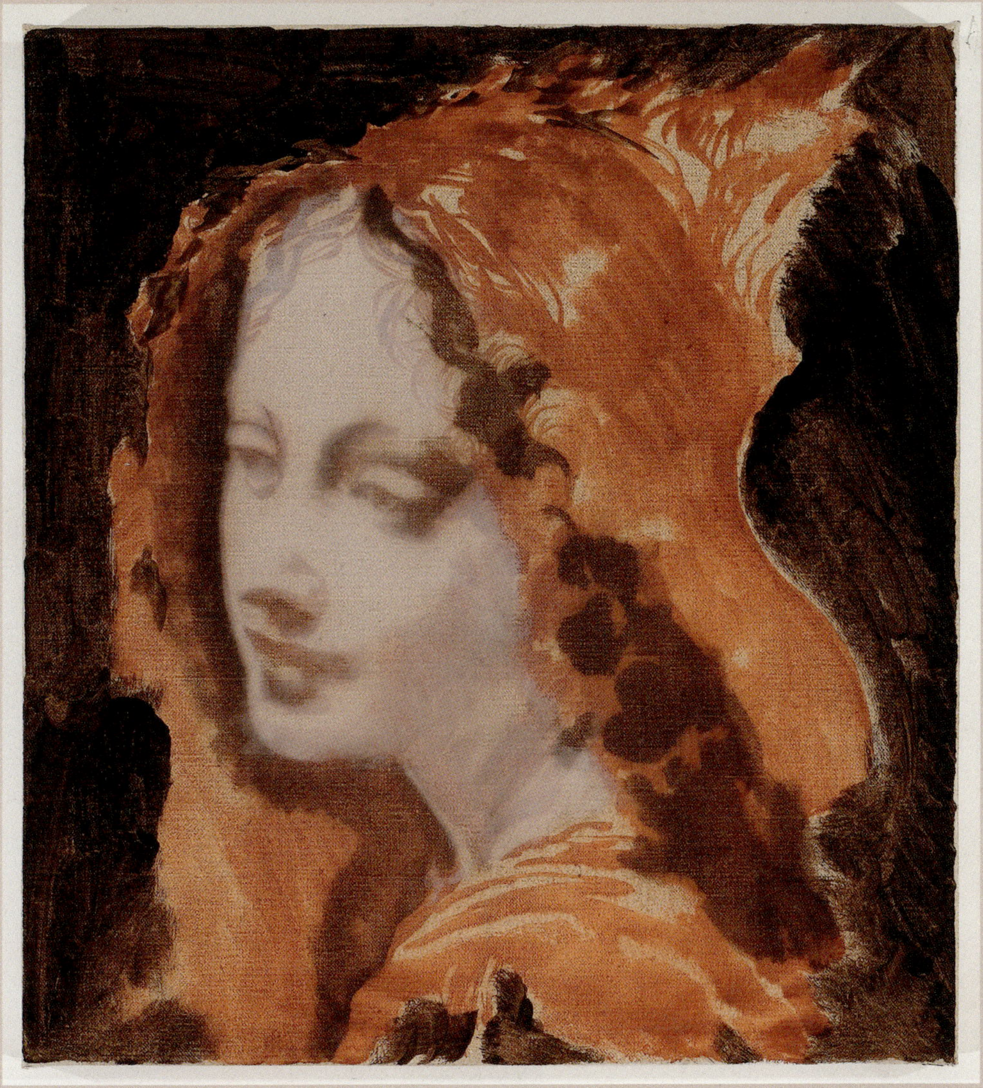

Angel, 2007
oil on linen, 38 x 35 cm
courtesy Newman Popiashvili Gallery, New York

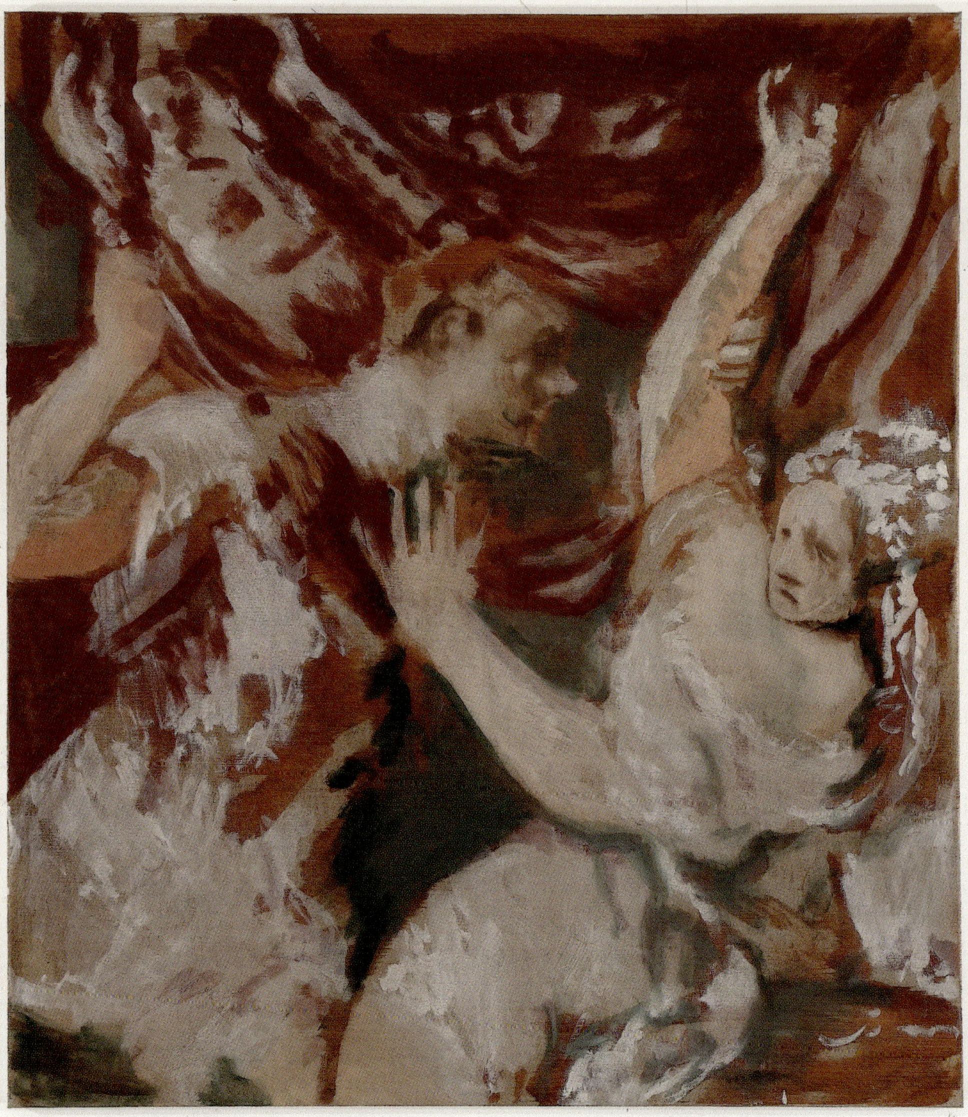

Tarquinius and Lucretia, 2007
oil on linen, 106 x 91 cm
collection the artist, New York

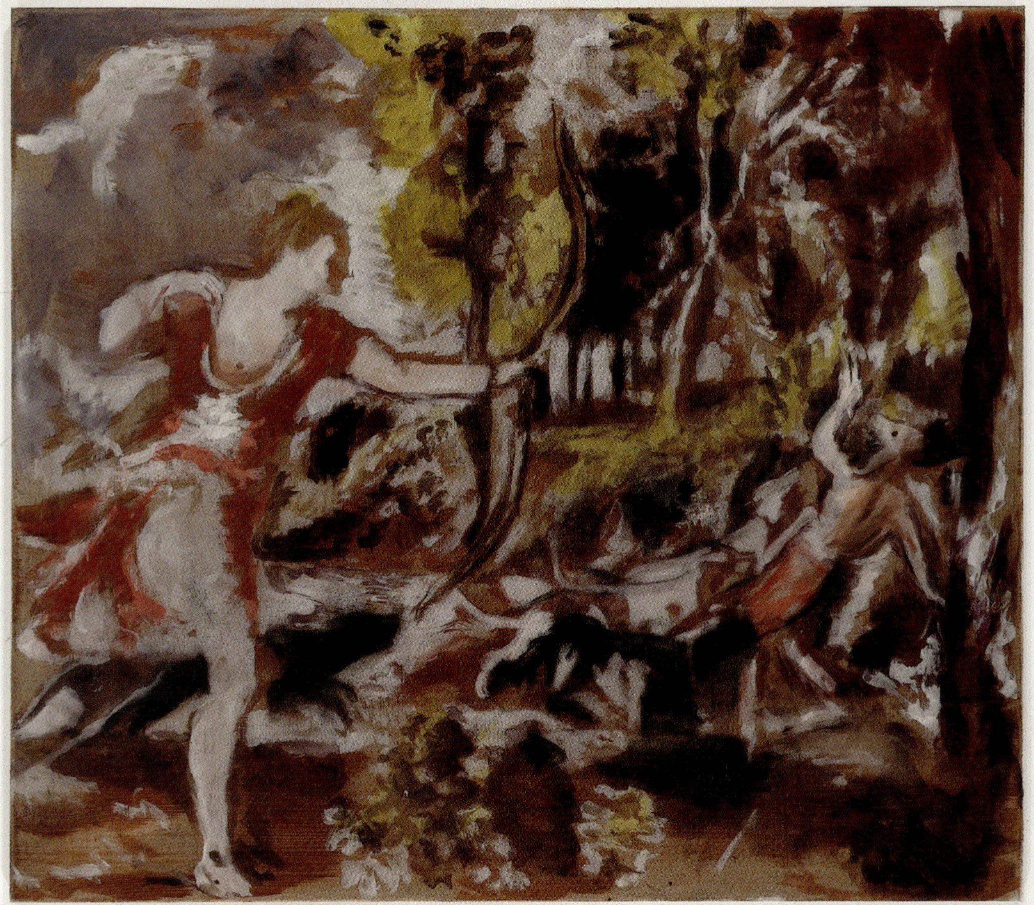

‘Kill that Bastard Actaeon’, 2007
oil on linen, 91 x 101,5 cm
collection the artist, New York

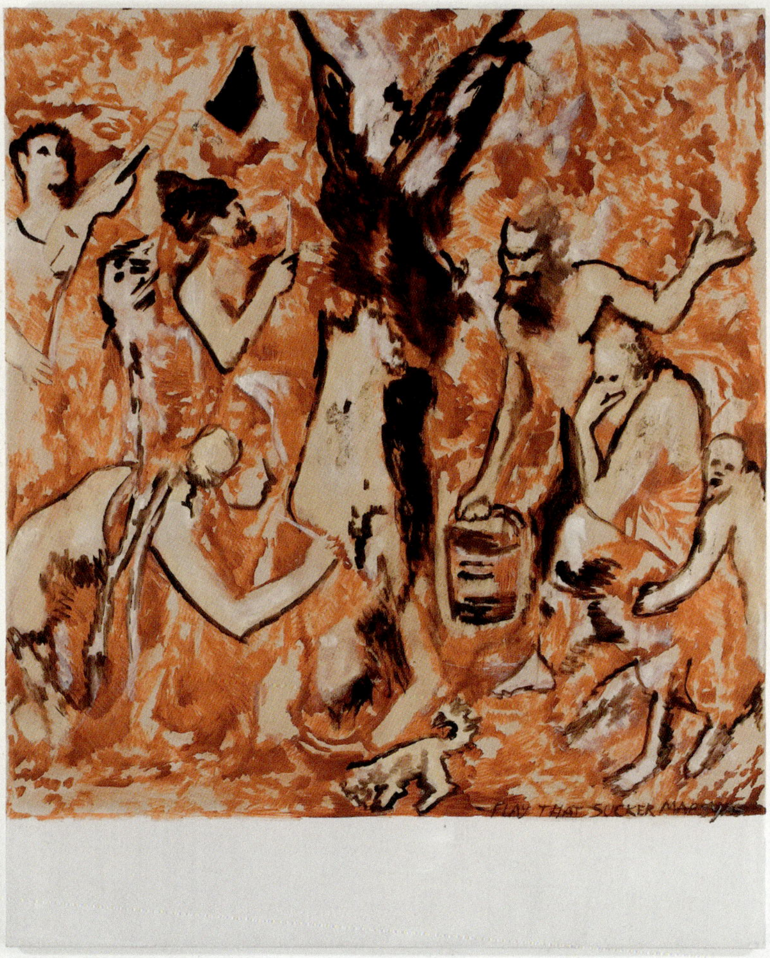

Flay that Sucker Marsyas, 2007
oil on linen, 200 x 160 cm
courtesy Galerie Tanya Rumpff, Haarlem, the Netherlands

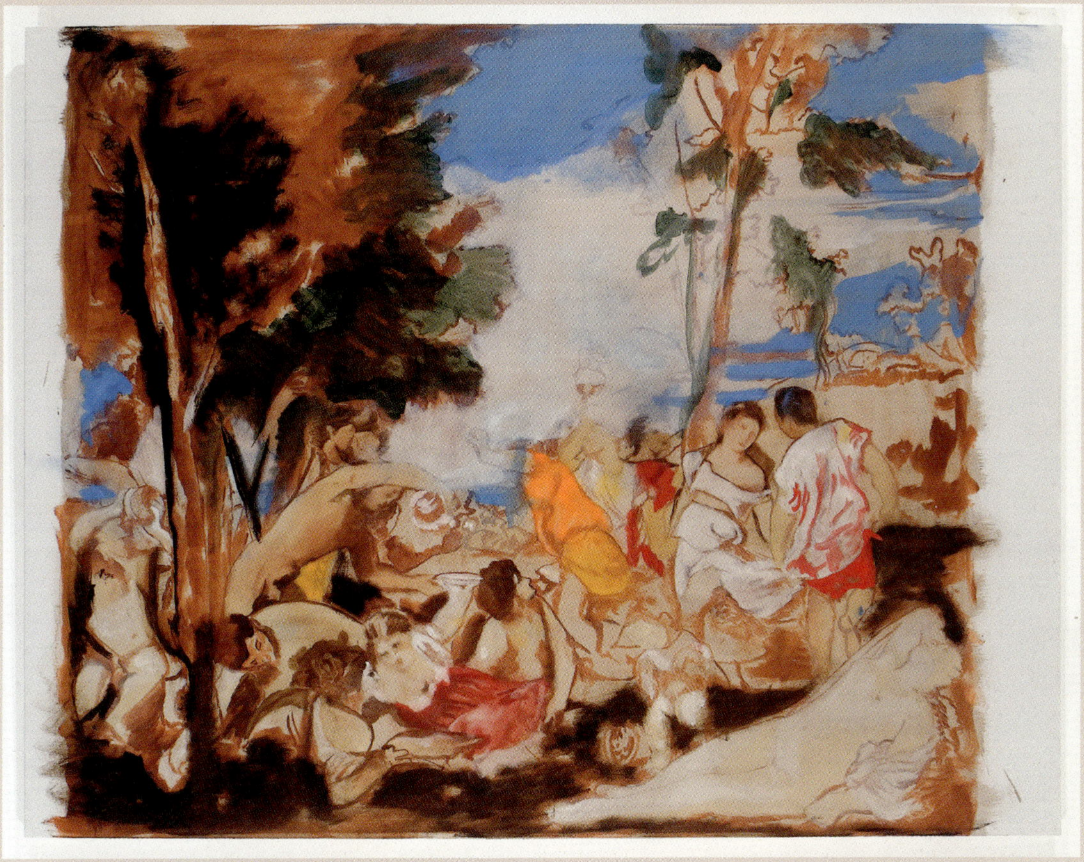

Party, 2007
oil on linen, 161 x 201 cm
courtesy Newman Popiashvili Gallery, New York

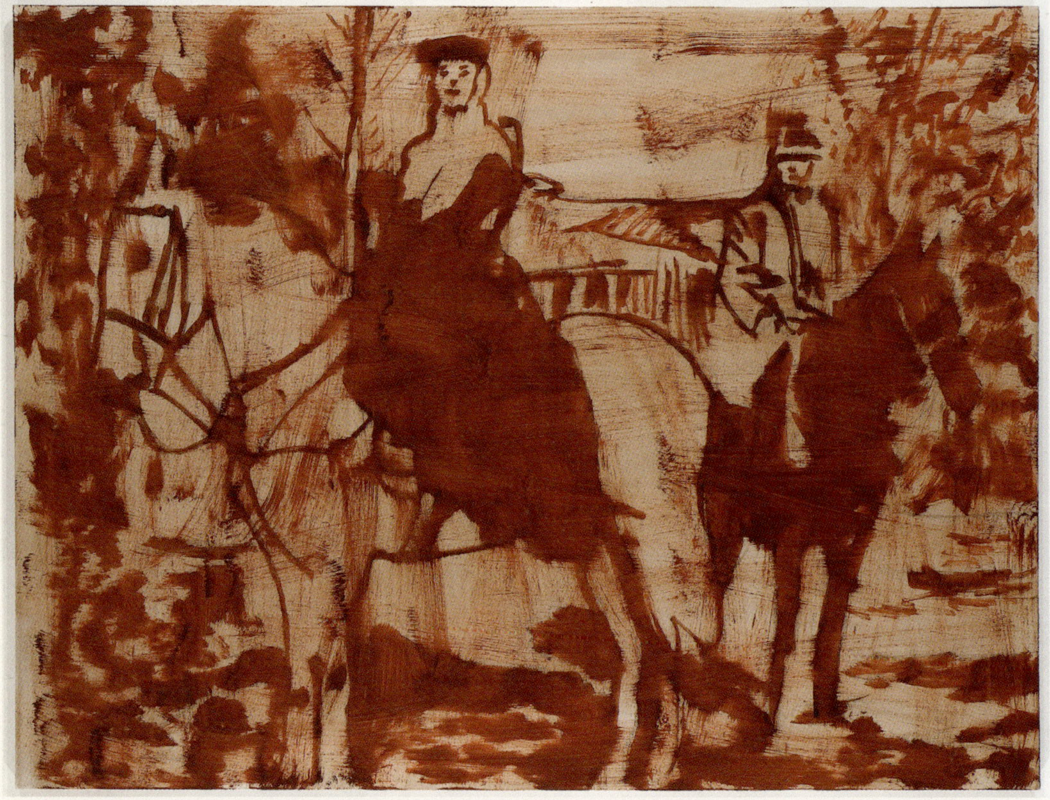

Portrait of Monica hunting, 2007
oil on linen, 155 x 201 cm
courtesy Newman Popiashvili Gallery, New York

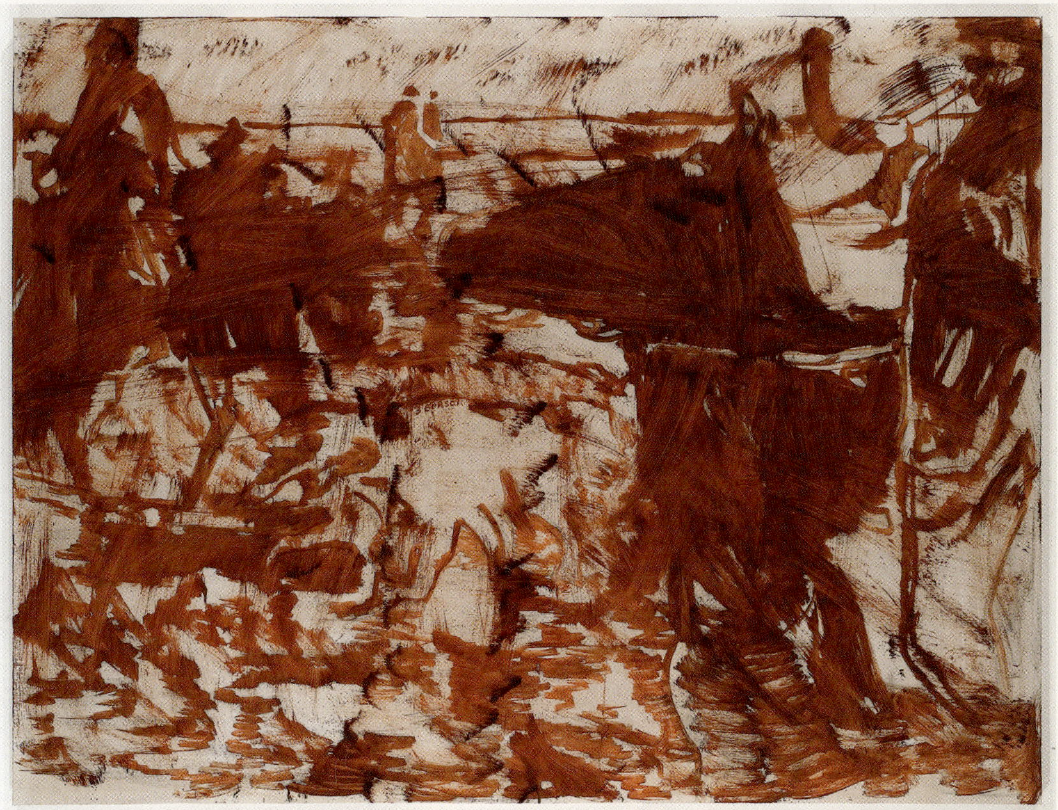

The Hunt, 2007
oil on linen, 155 x 201 cm
courtesy Newman Popiashvili Gallery, New York

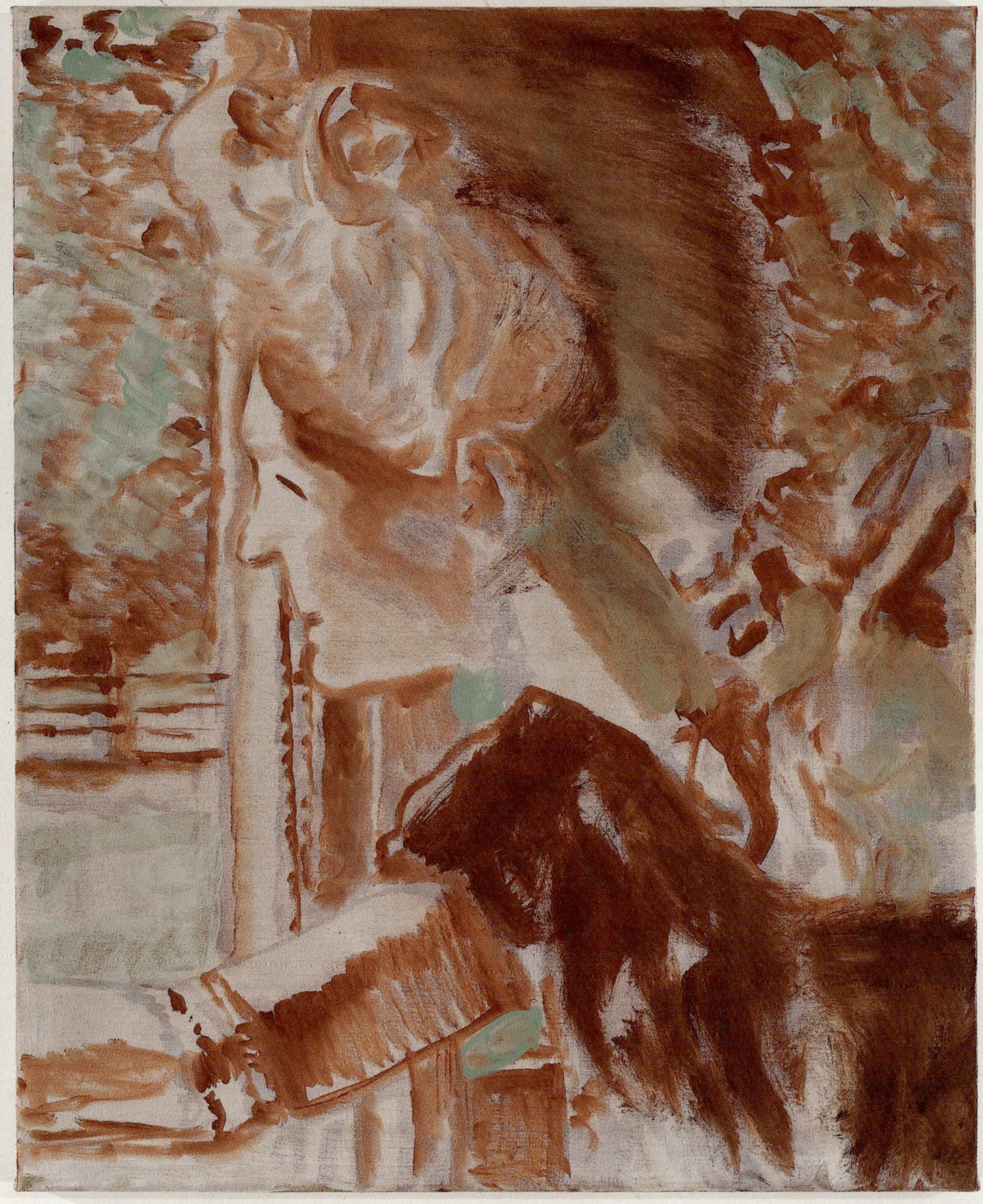

The Arrival, 2007
oil on linen, 76 x 60,5 cm
courtesy Galerie Tanya Rumpff, Haarlem, the Netherlands

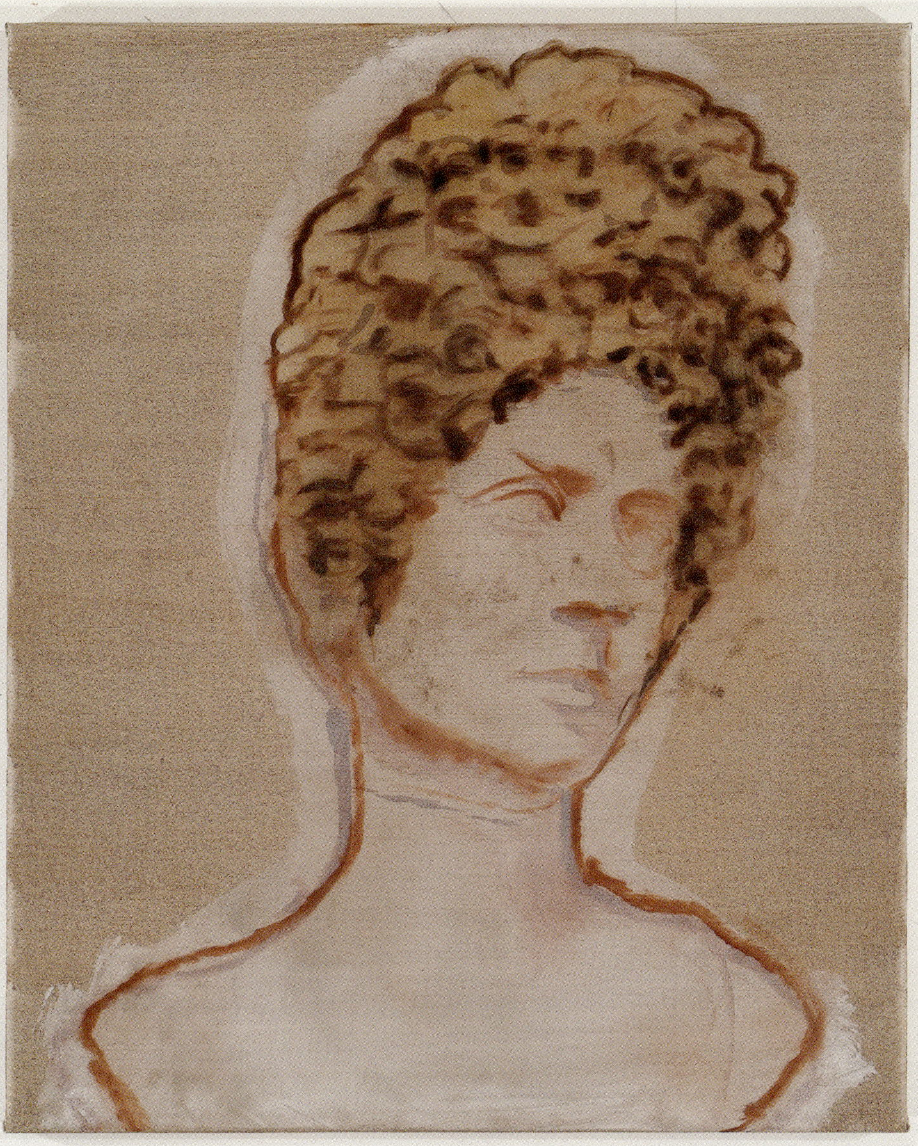

Roman Bust, 2007
oil on linen, 76 x 60,5 cm
collection the artist, New York

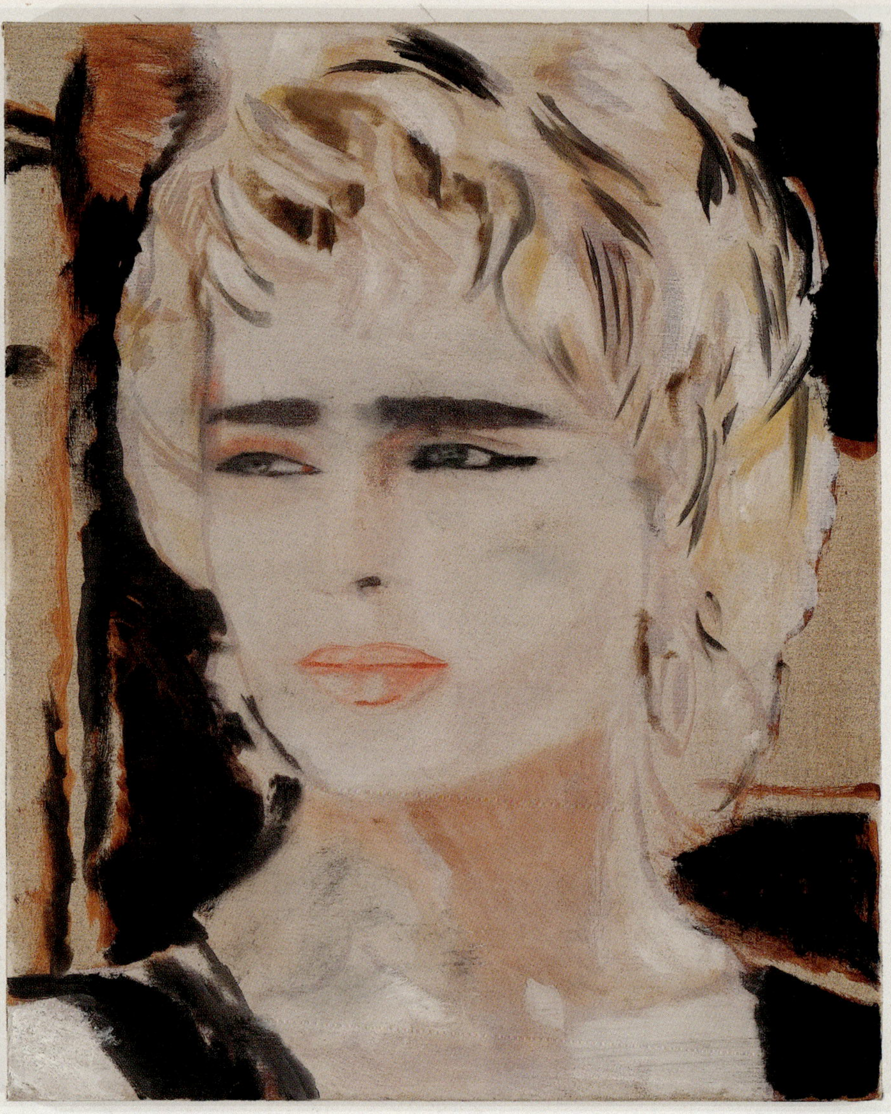

Isabella Rossellini, 2007
oil on linen, 76 x 60,5 cm
courtesy Galerie Tanya Rumpff, Haarlem, the Netherlands

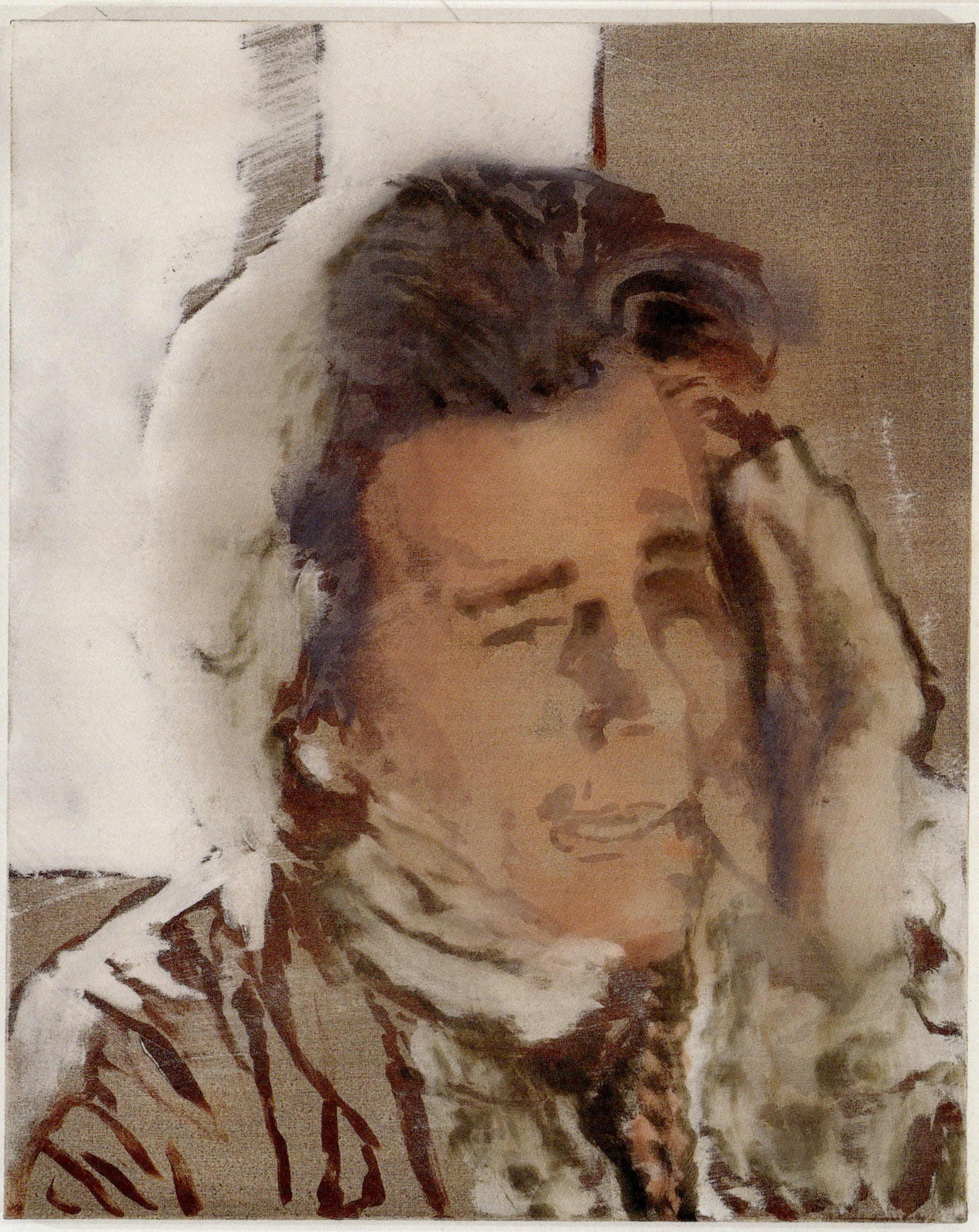

Self, 2006
oil on linen, 71 x 56 cm
collection the artist, New York

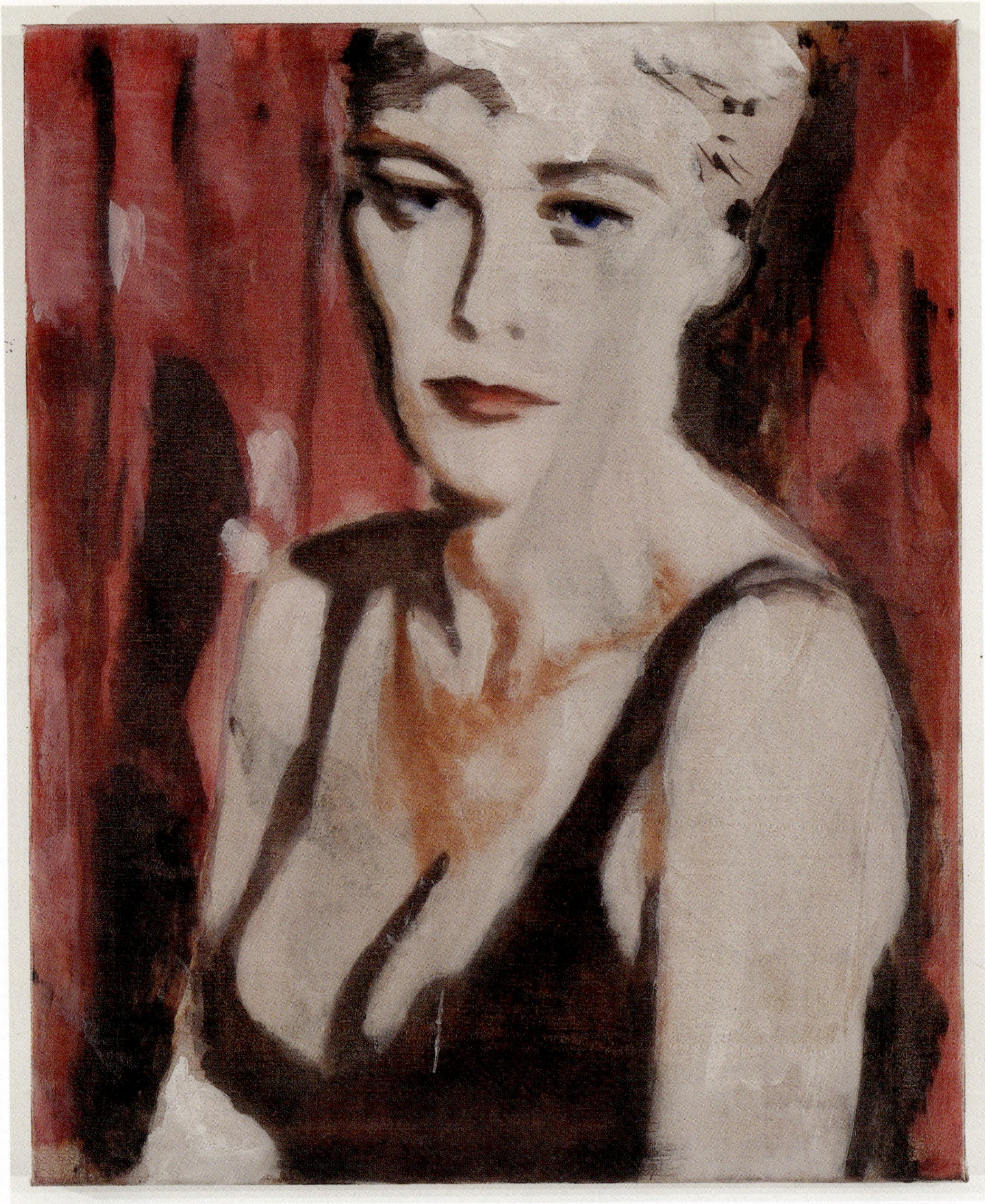

Teresa Banks, 2007
oil on linen, 76 x 61 cm
courtesy Galerie Tanya Rumpff, Haarlem, the Netherlands

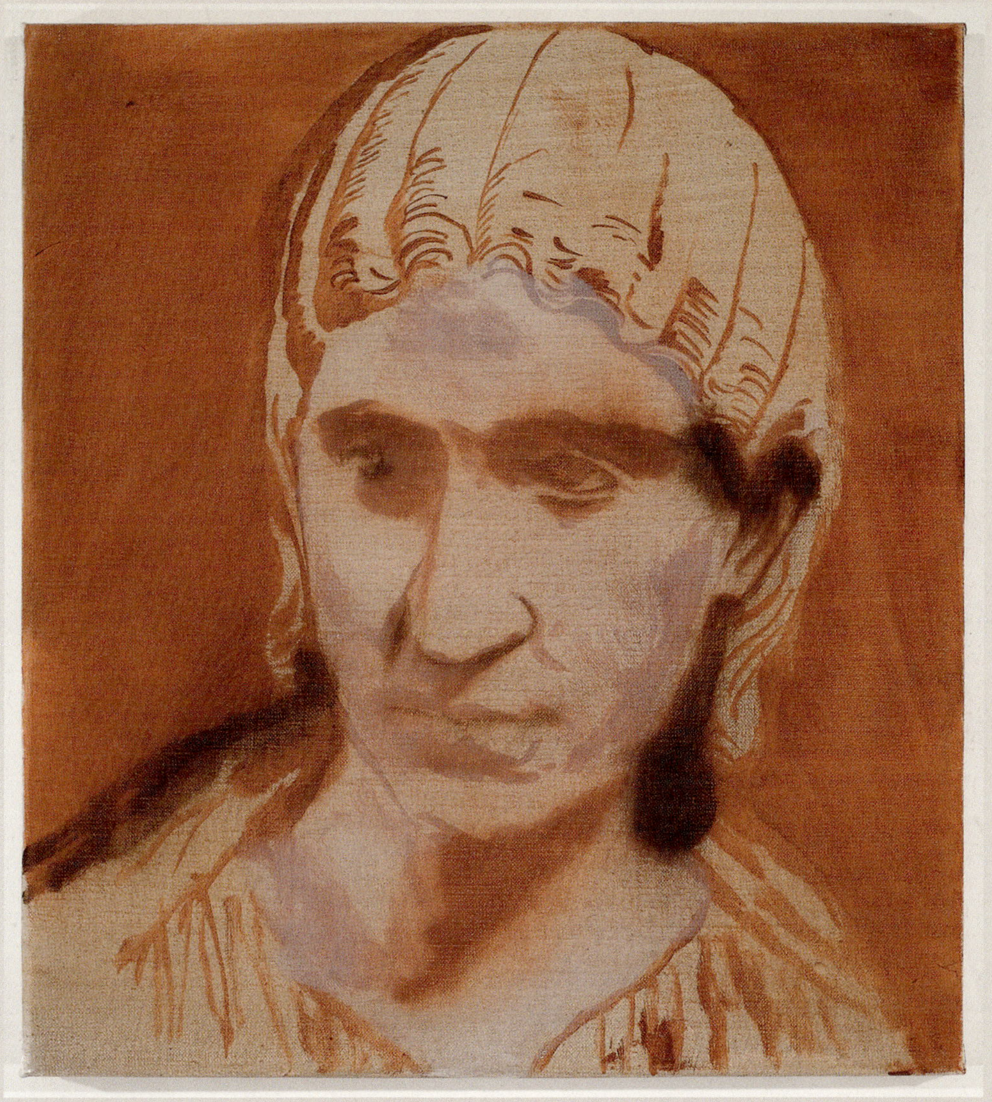

Julia Mamaea, 2007
oil on linen, 40,5 x 35 cm
courtesy Newman Popiashvili Gallery, New York

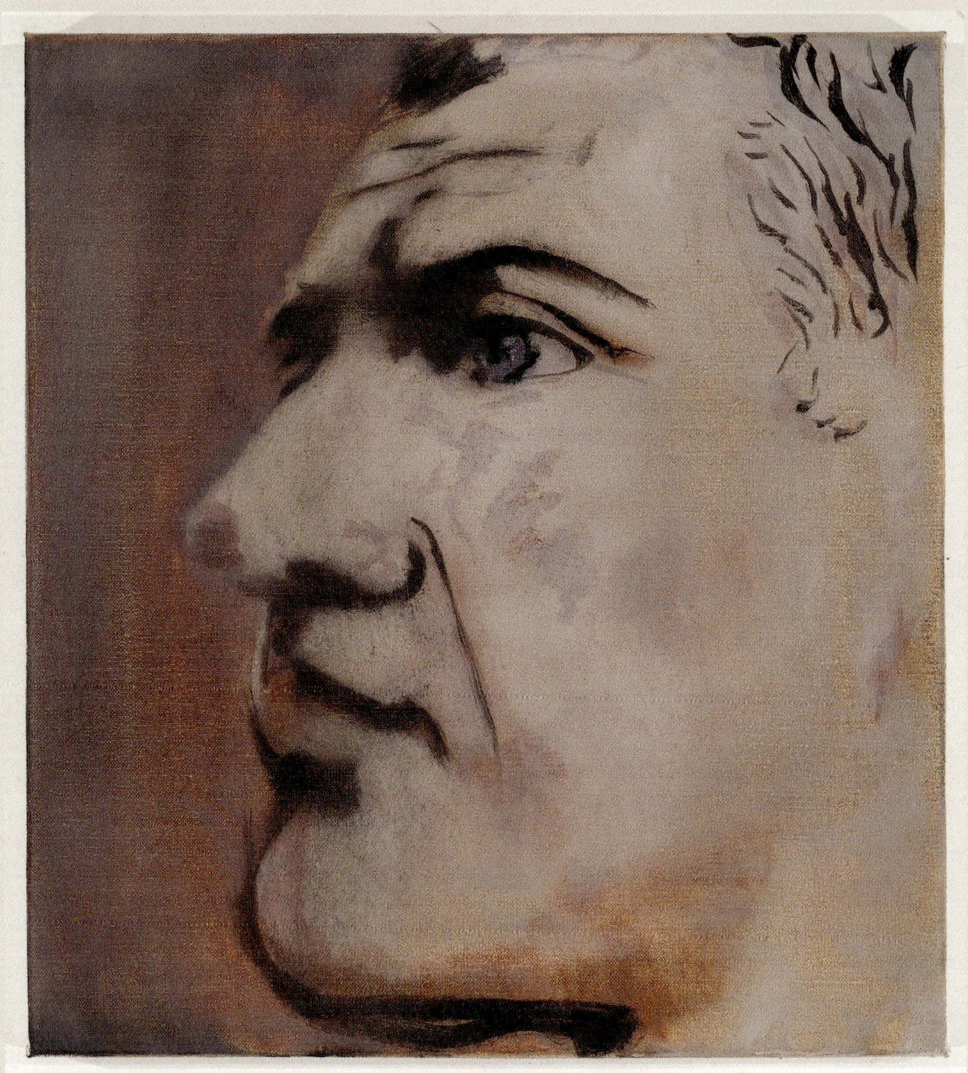

Caesar, 2007
oil on linen, 40,5 x 35,5 cm
courtesy Newman Popiashvili Gallery, New York

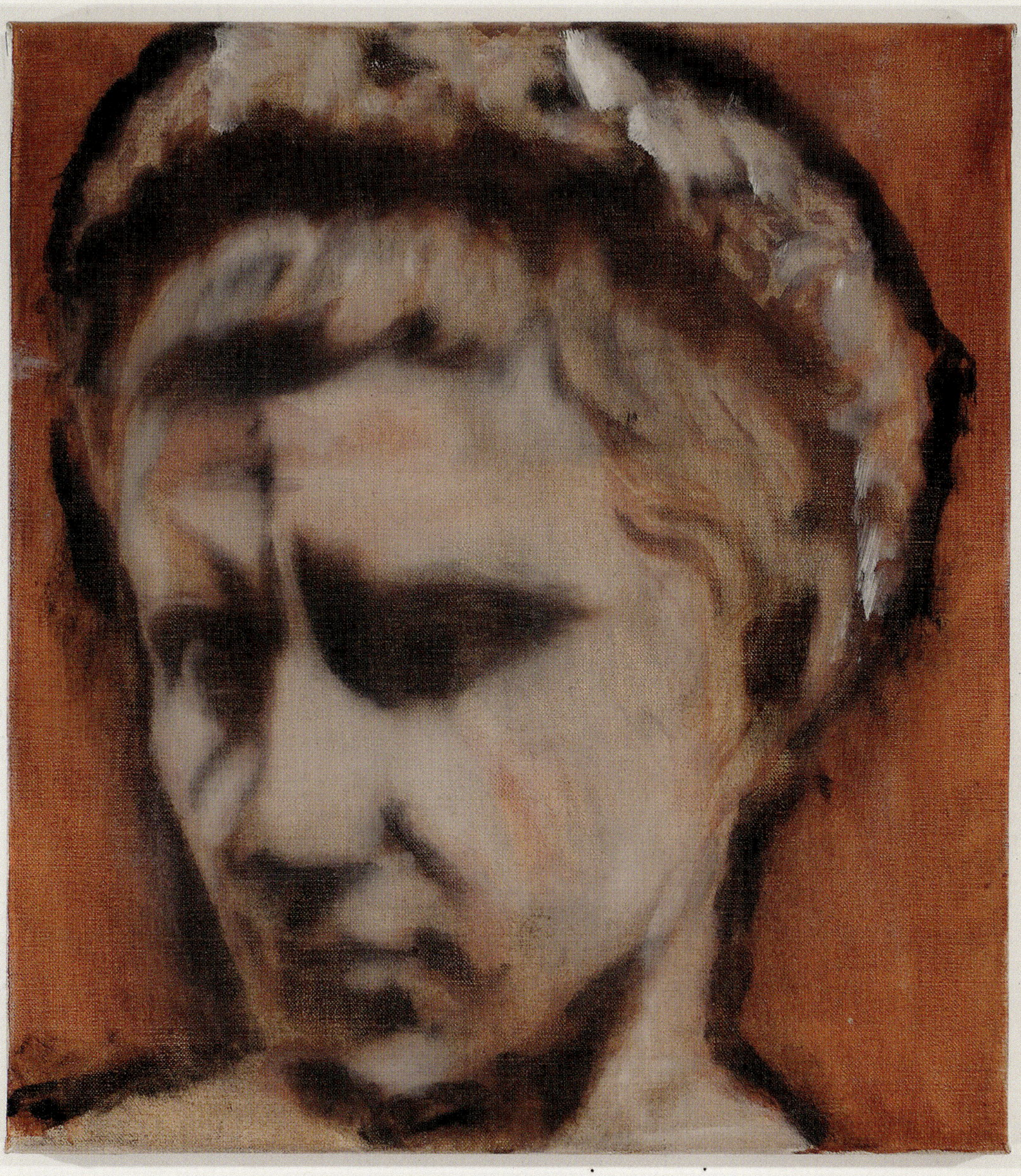

Augustus, 2007
oil on linen, 40,5 x 35 cm
courtesy Newman Popiashvili Gallery, New York

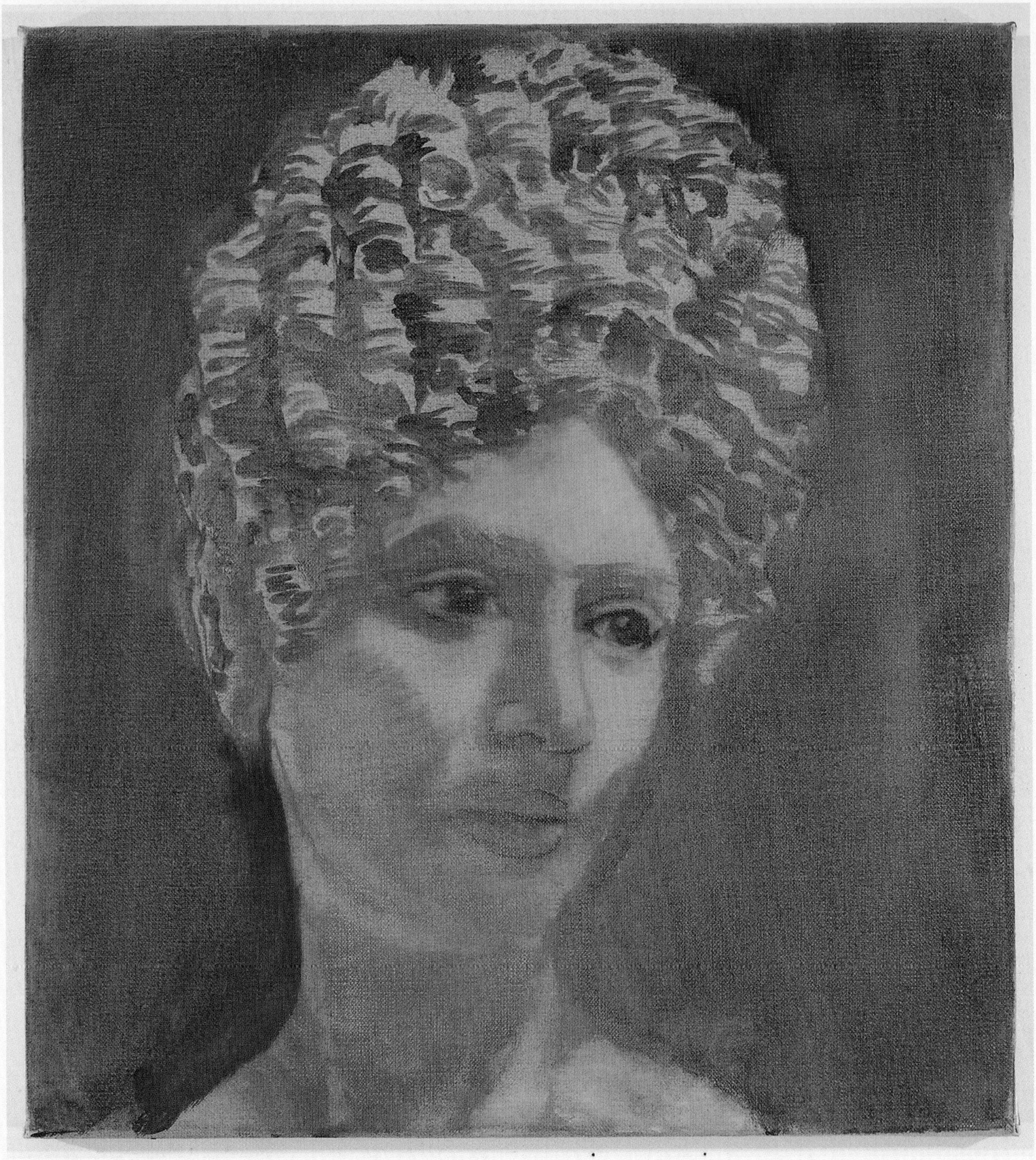

Portrait of a Lady, 2007
oil on linen, 40,5 x 35 cm
courtesy Newman Popiashvili Gallery, New York

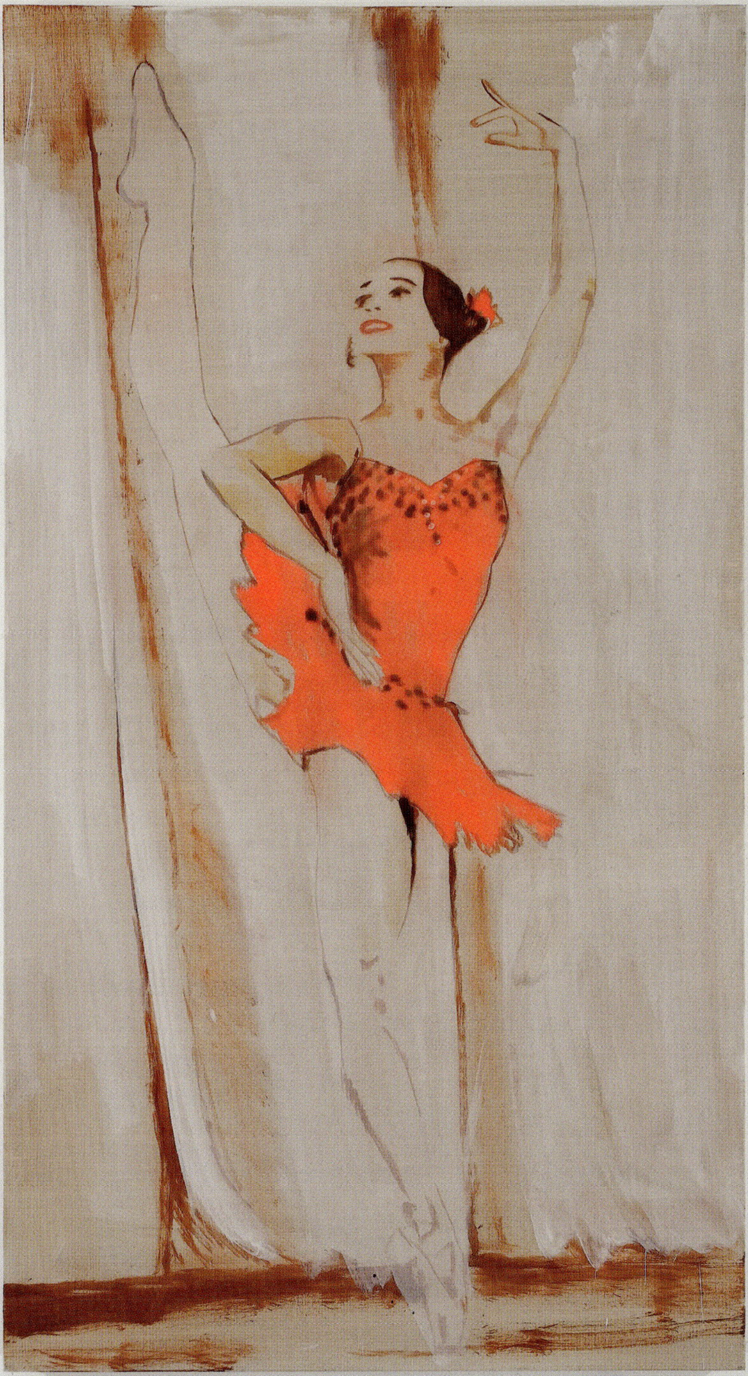

Nadezhda Pavlova, 2007
oil on linen, 173 x 91 cm
courtesy Galerie Tanya Rumpff, Haarlem, the Netherlands

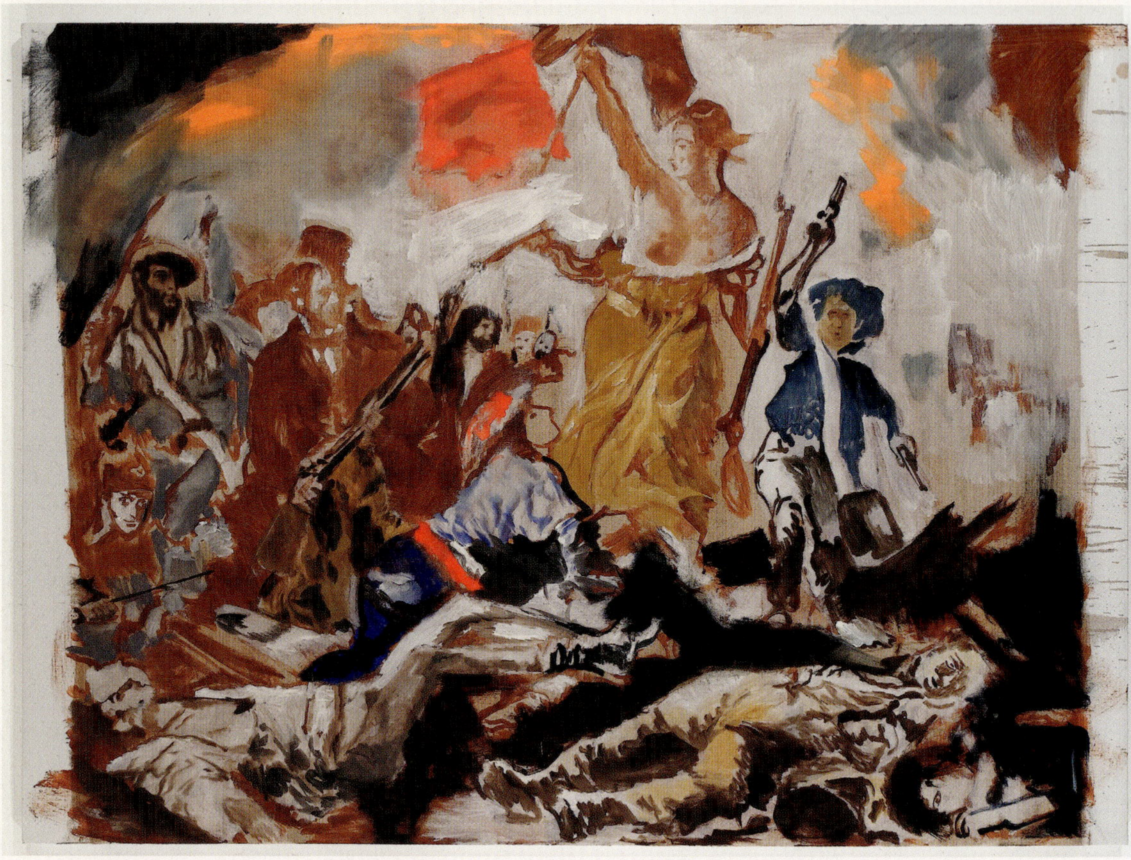

'Liberty' or 'Kill that Murderous Bunch', 2007
oil on linen, 151,5 x 200,5 cm
courtesy Galerie Tanya Rumpff, Haarlem, the Netherlands

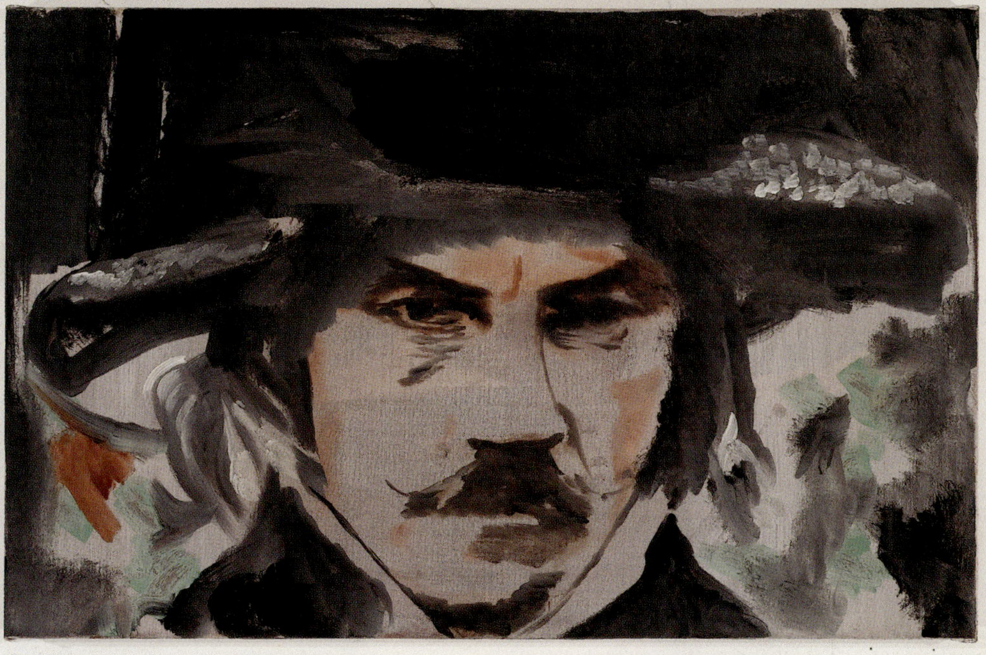

Lieutenant, 2007
oil on linen, 40,5 x 61 cm
courtesy Newman Popiashvili Gallery, New York

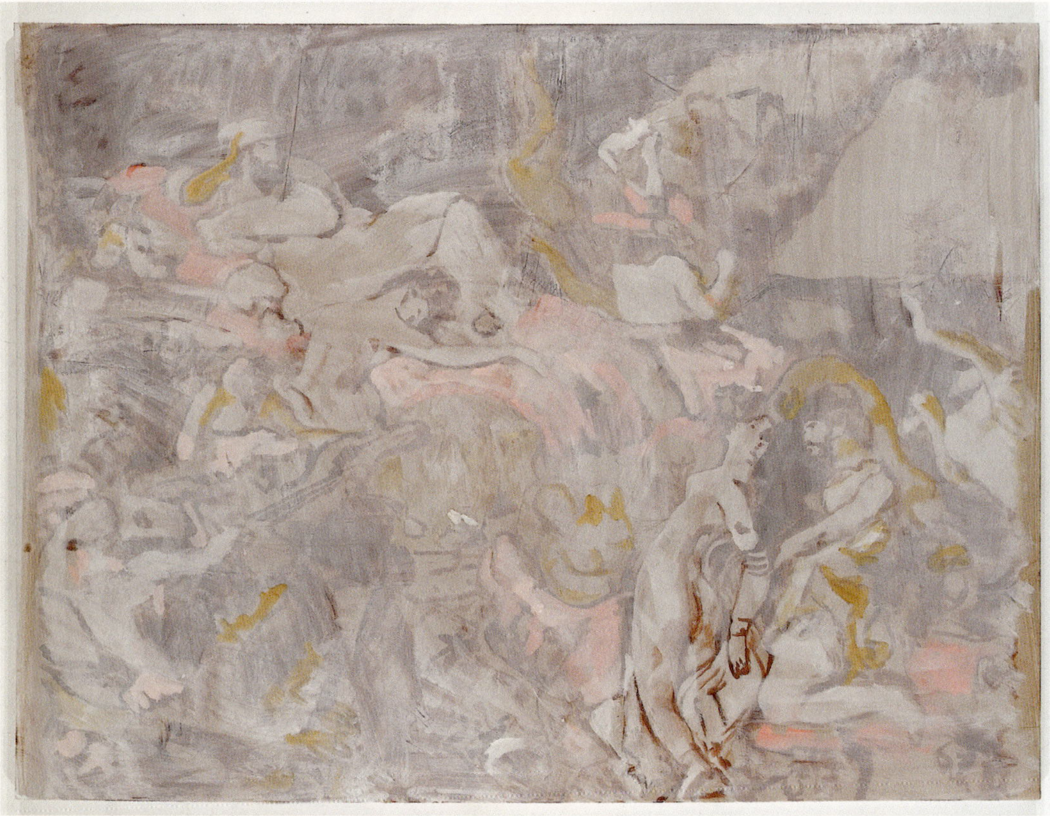

Suicide, 2007
oil on linen, 157,5 x 200,5 cm
courtesy Galerie Tanya Rumpff, Haarlem, the Netherlands

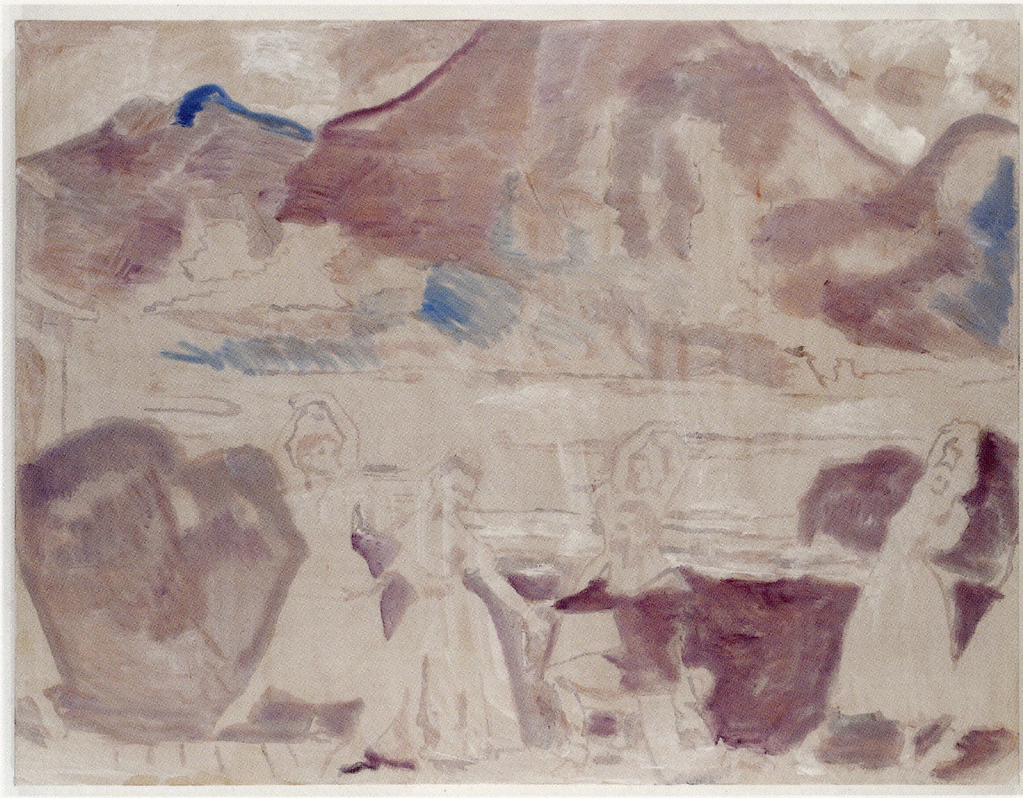

Dance, 2007
oil on linen, 155,5 x 201 cm
courtesy Galerie Tanya Rumpff, Haarlem, the Netherlands

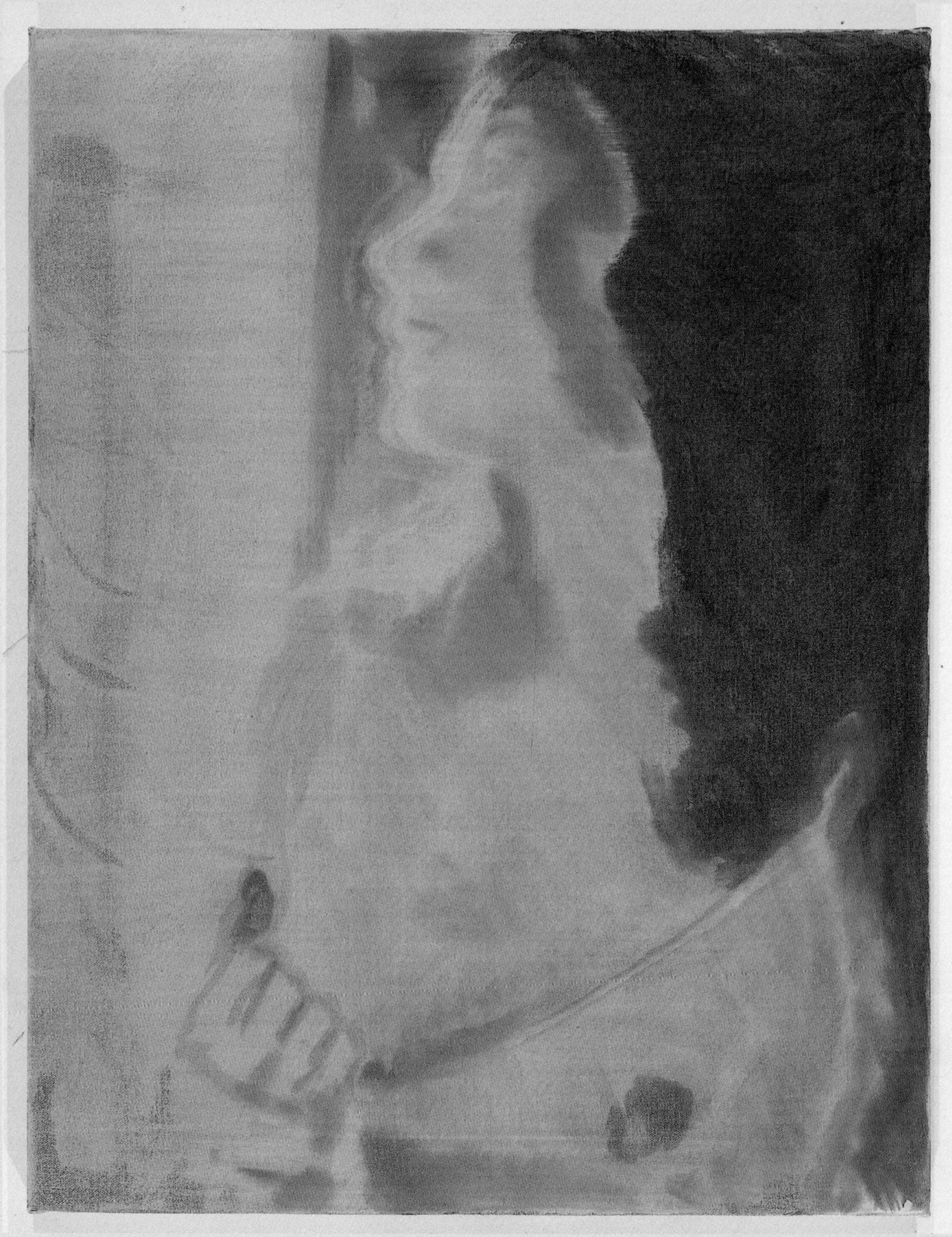

Male Gaze nr 1, 2007
oil on linen, 60,5 x 45,5 cm
courtesy Newman Popiashvili Gallery, New York

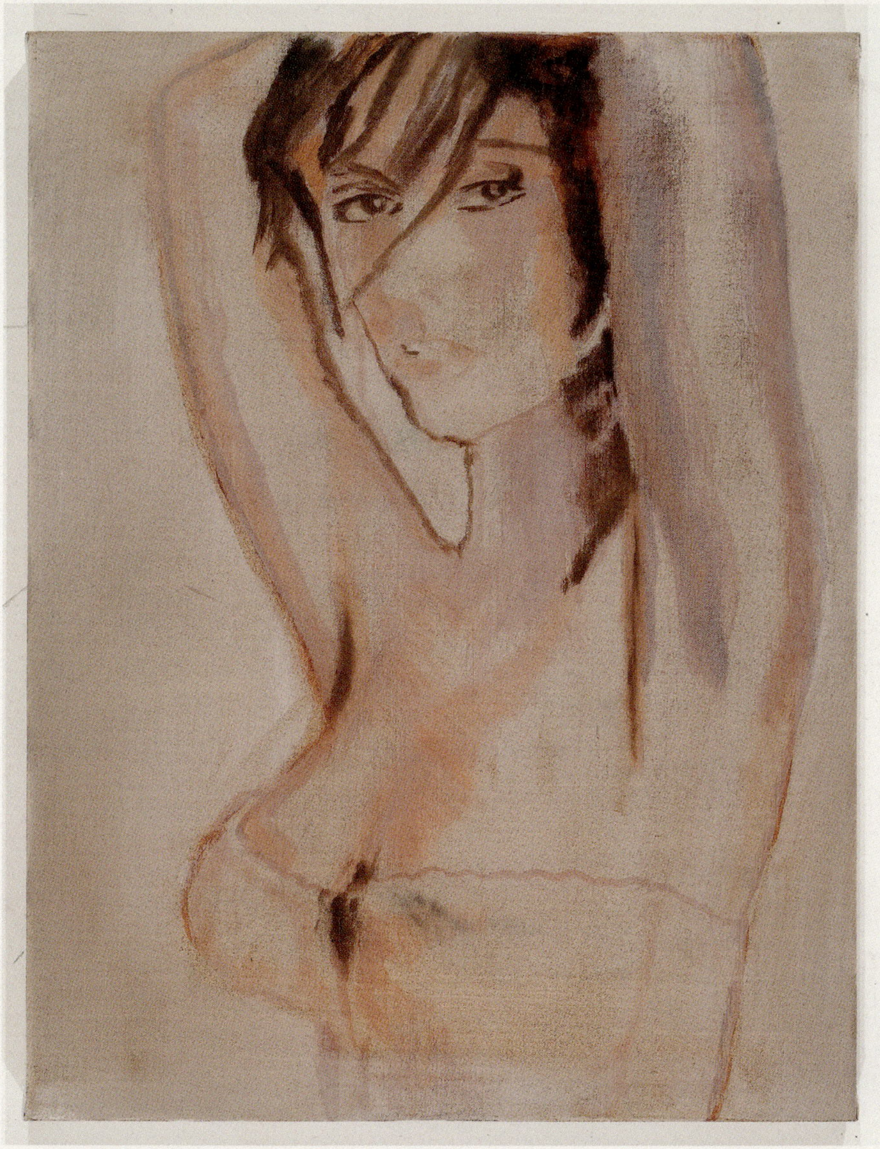

Male Gaze nr 2, 2007
oil on linen, 60,5 x 45,5 cm
courtesy Galerie Tanya Rumpff, Haarlem, the Netherlands

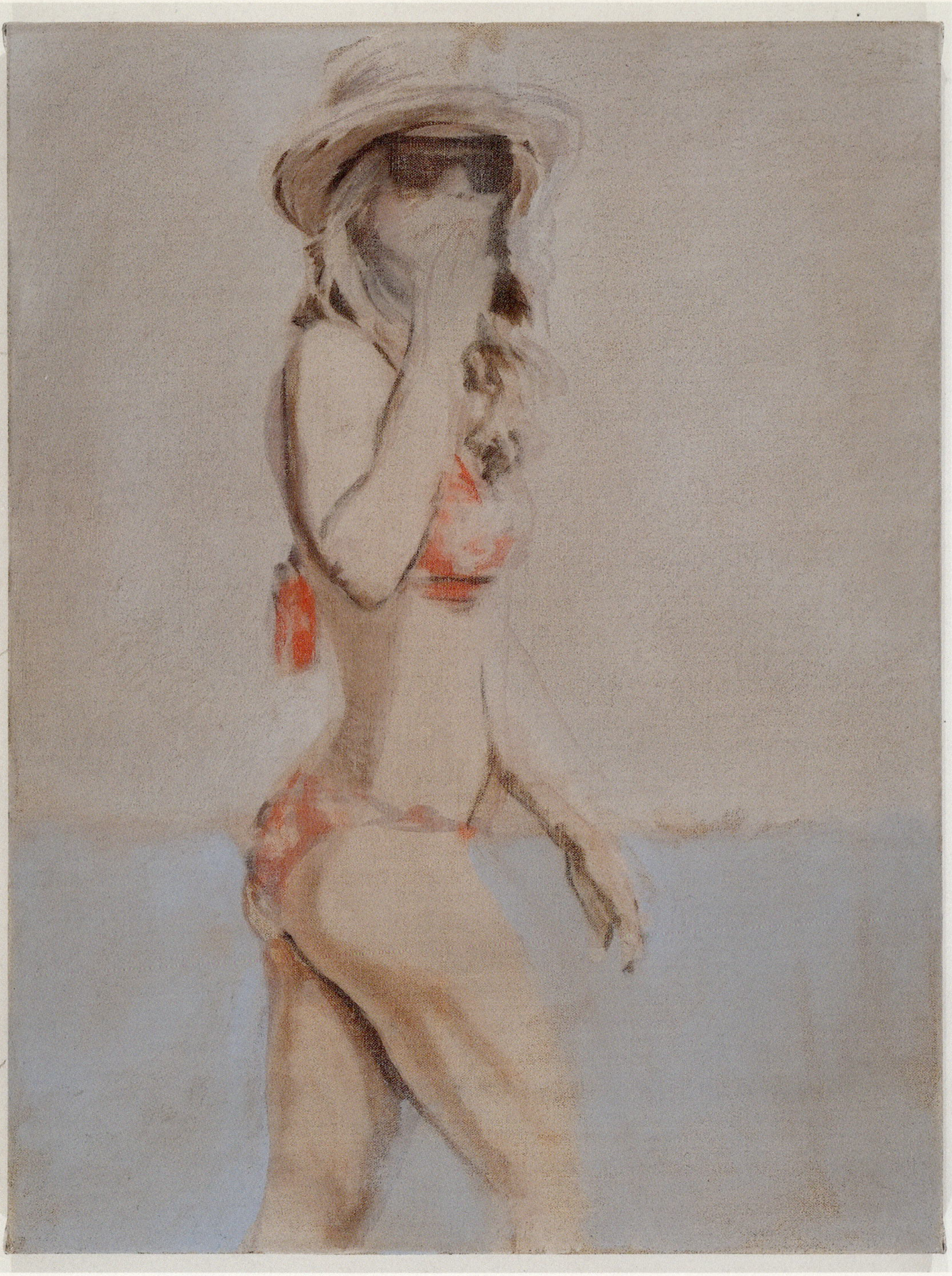

Beach Photo, 2007
oil on linen, 60,5 x 45,5 cm
courtesy Newman Popiashvili Gallery, New York

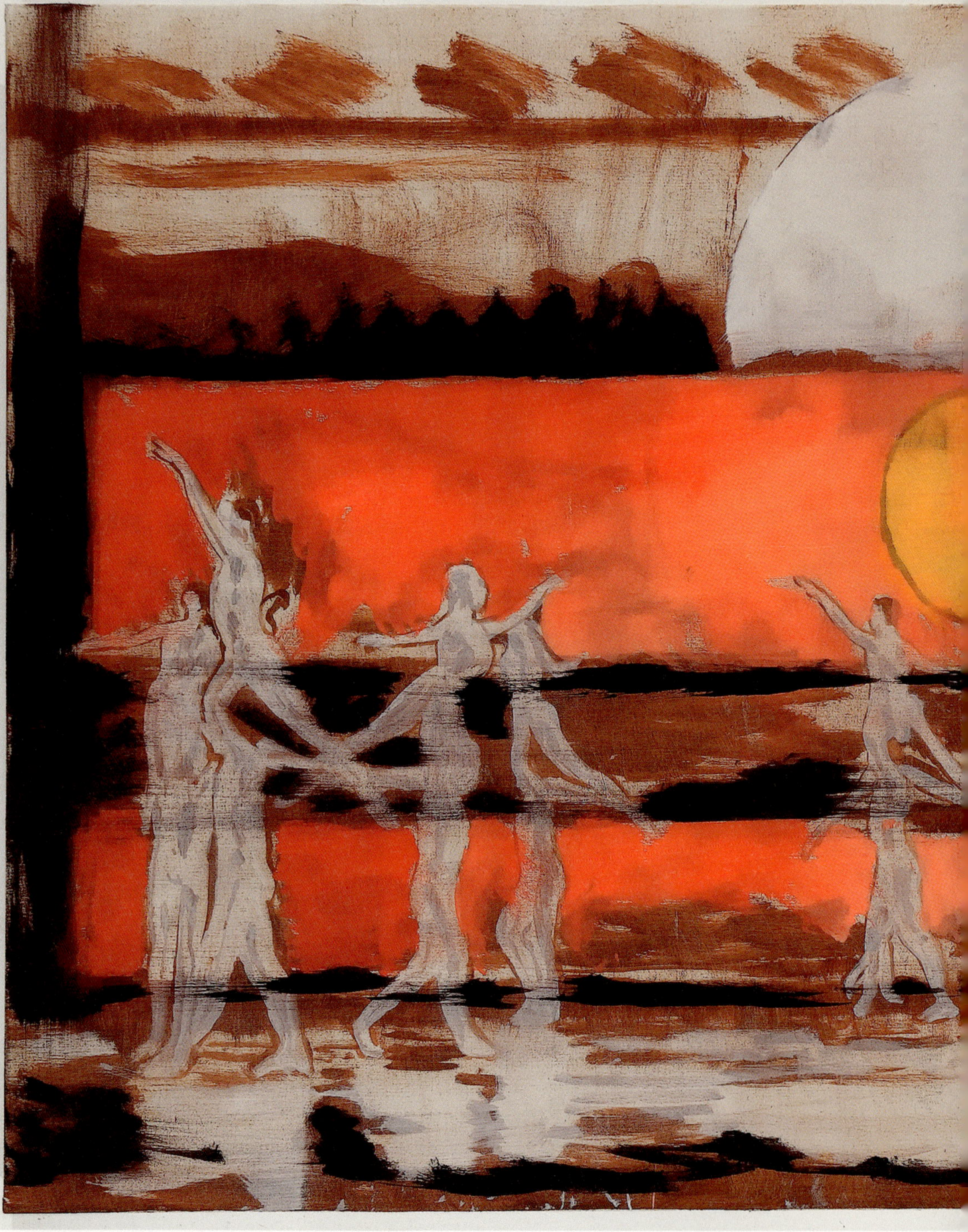

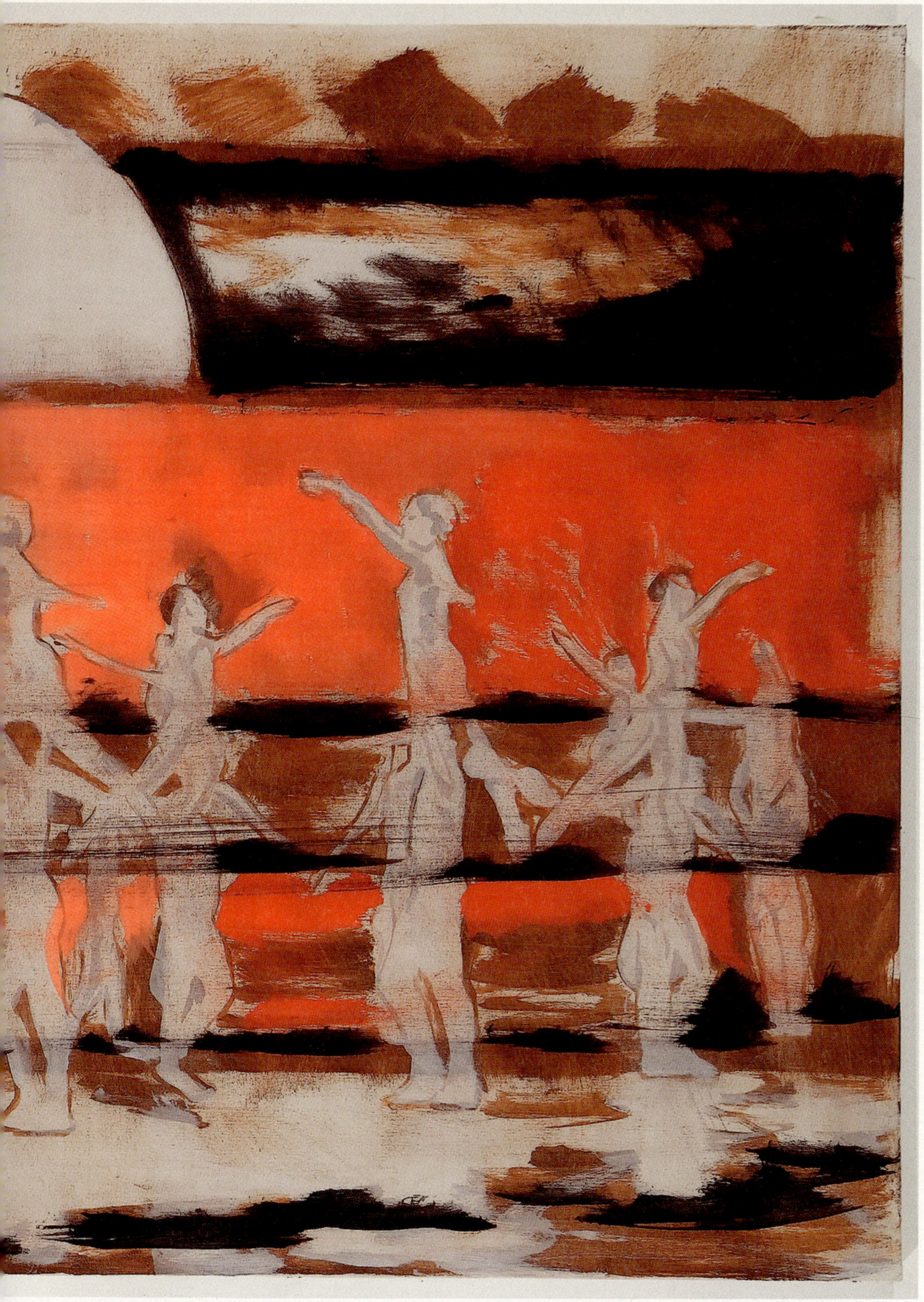

Turangalila, 2007
oil on linen, 125 x 200 cm
collection the artist, New York

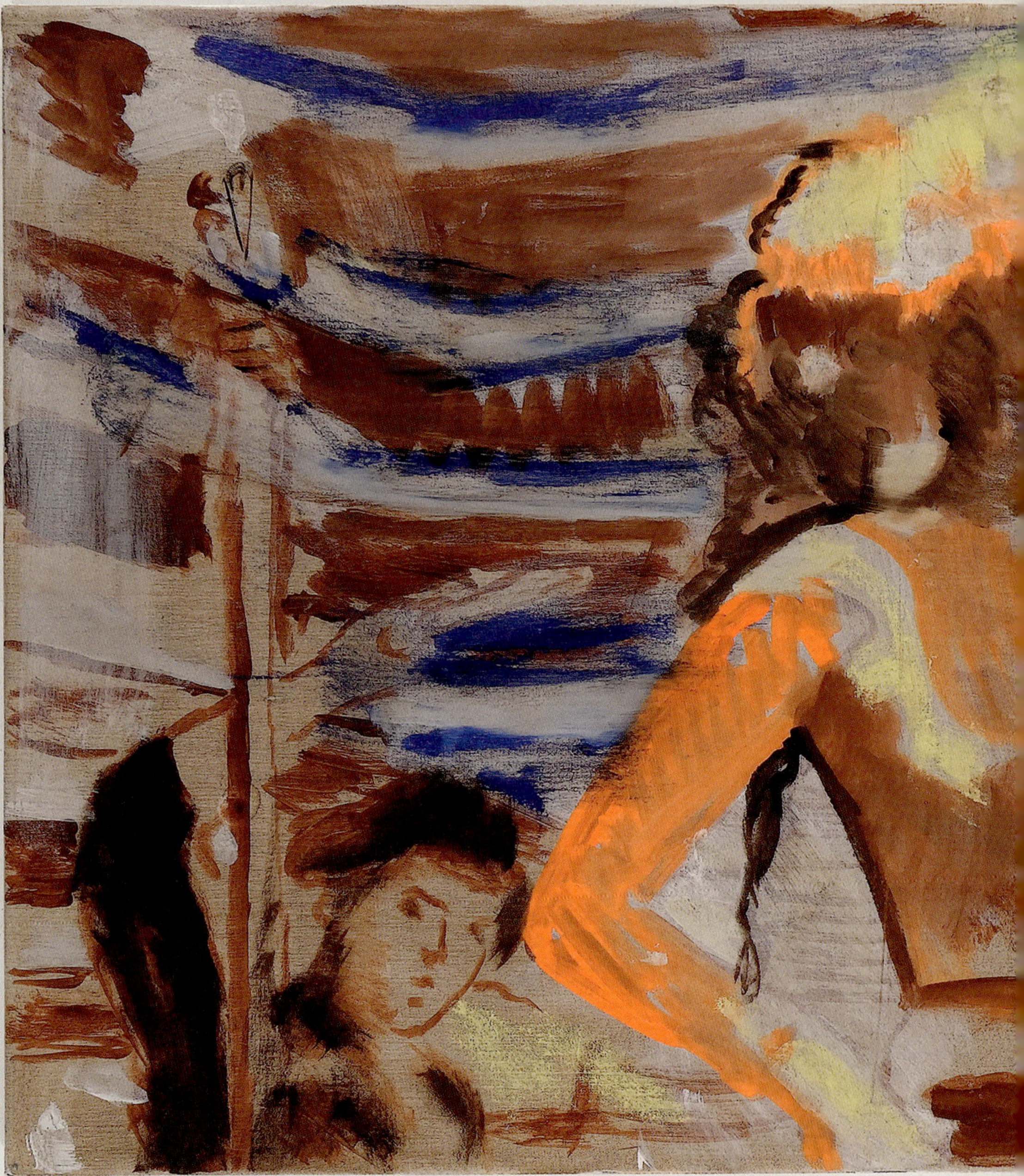

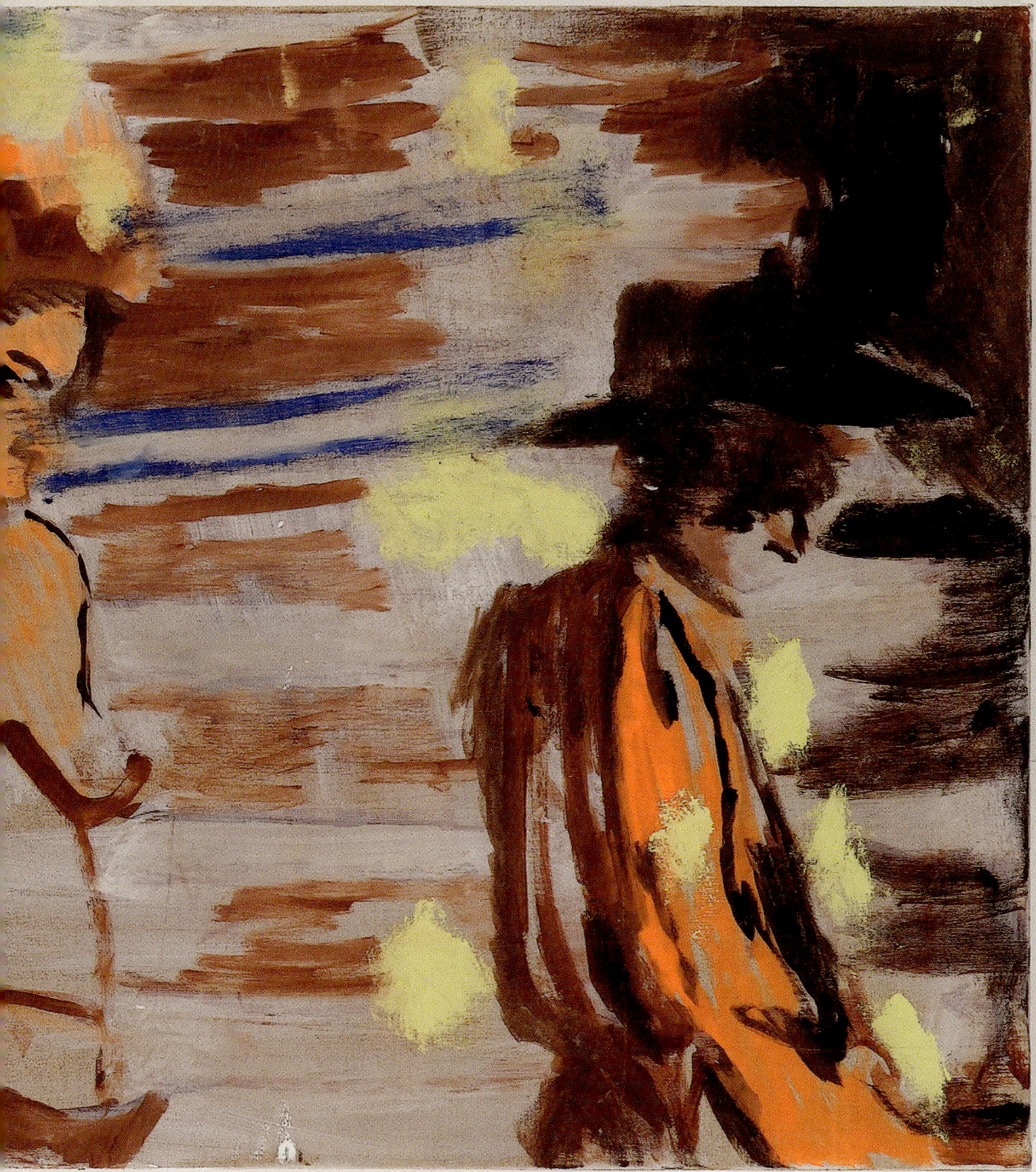

Stage, 2007
oil on linen, 75 x 137,5 cm
courtesy Galerie Tanya Rumpff, Haarlem, the Netherlands

Hans Broek: Old Faces, New Impressions

by Jennie Hirsh

Dutch painter Hans Broek established himself in the United States as a landscape painter focused on the city of Los Angeles, the artist's home from 1995 until 2005.

But since relocating to New York City two years ago, Broek has radically altered the style, subject, and scope of his work. No longer generating the cool, restrained geometric compositions of the glittering hills of LA and the inherently artificial aesthetic of California life, he has embarked upon an appropriative artistic adventure characterized by loose brushwork and stained planes of color that take the viewer on a Grand Tour of the history of representation. Broek's present pictorial project relies on a range of sources that are themselves iconic images. Moving from the paintings of Leonardo Da Vinci, Titian, and Diego Velasquez to the films of Sergei Bondarchuk, Stanley Kubrick, and David Lynch, Broek's current body of work is a series of pictorial translations drawn from traditions as diverse as antique sculpture, Old Master paintings, landmark films and even images of historically significant theatrical, musical, and dance performances. His multi-media inspiration includes a wide array of themes and subjects including portraiture, genre scenes, classical mythology, religious iconography, and historical fiction. Having abandoned the mechanical discipline of his earlier facture, he has become an artistic archaeologist who excavates perennial elements of human behavior from an ever-growing inventory of painters, sculptors, filmmakers, and photographers. In creating new impressions of old faces, Broek has abandoned his disciplined Apollonian artistry in favor of an exuberant Dionysiac phase in which he resurrects the power of painter and subject in Janus-faced compositions that speak to both the past and the present.

But before turning to the individual works themselves, I should say a few words about the premise of Broek's pictorial project. What consistently informs the artist's current practice is his incisive ability to enter into and excavate energy from images as poignant and diverse as Titian's *Flaying of Marsyas* (1523-25), Eugene Delacroix's *Liberty Leading the People* (1830) and Sergei Bondarchuk's *War and Peace* (1968). Themes of revolution and revelry alike stand out in Broek's representations of the perpetual predicaments of the human condition, as he highlights universal tensions that exceed geographical and chronological bounds. Self-consciously imprecise copies of compositions that are to greater and lesser extents readily recognizable, his paintings abstract the political, sexual, and biological drives that underline all human behavior in his signature pictorial language infused with topical themes such as death, desire, and destruction.

Ancient Faces, New Facture

Painterly reproductions of ancient Roman portraits, whether comments on sculpted imperial busts or mysterious painted panel portraits of Fayum, represent a key component of Broek's project. The loosely painted crown of curls of *Portrait of a Lady* (2007) conjures up associations with imperial portraits of women of the Antonine dynasty as well as more modern coiffures, ranging from late eighteenth-century French wigs to the bouffant hairstyle popular in the late 1950s and 1960s and even the contemporary cartoon character Marge Simpson. Complicating these multiple connections is the title *Portrait of a Lady*, which imparts a nineteenth-century sensibility to the ancient figurehead by alluding to Henry James' novel of the same name, which first appeared in serial form in *The Atlantic Monthly* between 1880 and 1881 and was itself the subject of a film adaptation by Jane Campion in 1996. *Julia Mamaea* (2007), a powerful female figure in the Severan dynasty, adds yet another dimension to the critical side of this series. An androgynous paraphrase of imperial portraits of this influential woman, Broek's *Julia* is not readily legible as a female figure. Her heavy eyebrows and square jaw appear masculine, while her synthetic-looking rows of curls recall the patterns of late eighteenth-century wigs for men. Blurring the limits of gender and history underscores not only the instability of pictorial signs but also the potency of Broek's extraction process itself.

Augustus (2007), a take-off on a marble portrait of the first emperor, offers another curious example of the artist's appropriative improvisations. Whereas the point of reference for this painting was a polished, and, in that sense, finished bust, what results on the surface of this canvas is something incomplete. In other words, Broek, the contemporary painter, turns back the clock as he returns the ancient sculpture to an earlier moment in its life as the form barely emerges from the rough stone. In so doing, Broek substitutes his artistic hand for that of the "original" artist; paradoxically, his finishing touches take away from rather than add to the execution of the piece. This subtractive gesture opens up the artwork for increased psychological presence in the absence of fixed physical aspect. Trapped between photography and painting, citation and parody, the ambiguous texture and hue of *Augustus* resist immediate identification, deflating the monumentality of such portraiture (and perhaps such leaders) through a spray paint-like rendition of a perplexed emperor whose strange pallor and dusty surface belies his pictorial predicament.

Making Amends

Both *Monica Hunting* (2007) and *The Hunt* (2007), drawn from Sergei Bondarchuk's 1968 film adaptation of Leo Tolstoy's *War and Peace*, initiate another adaptation of this epic tale. In converting film, a time-based medium, into paint, a static one, Broek reduces a colorful frame in which the story's heroine Natasha Rostova – here played by a former lover of the artist – sits on horseback frozen in a reflective moment during a hunt. Broek hastily sketches the essential elements of the scene, concentrating the anticipation of the moment in the staunch posture of the human figures and the fixed musculature of the ready horses. Measuring five by seven feet, this monumental image confronts the viewer with loose but deliberate brushwork in a sepia palette that masquerades as a study for an even larger scale mural work.

But if *Monica Hunting* expresses restrained potential energy, then *The Hunt* (2007) is its antidote. Here Broek unleashes the action of the hunt through facture that comes to the fore, nearly erasing the narrative content of the scene. Overwriting the image to the point of obliterating it, the paint, antagonistically applied in wide brushstrokes, invites a dual reading. *Hunt* not only foregrounds painting as a performance charged with the emotion of abstract expressionism, but also mimetically gestures toward the frenzied experience of both hunter and hunted when they are in the thick of it. Thus, he effectively reduces the conflict to a mass of geometric forms at odds with one another, echoing the patchy, earth-toned color field canvases of Clyfford Still. Broek mines and refracts the energy of the action at hand in a dynamic composition that captures the universal impulses that motivate any killing craze. By extension then, *Hunt* becomes symbolic of large-scale battles complete with pillaging perpetrators and harried victims. In staging the physical friction between discordant directives of paint, Broek also stages a second violent battle, between paint and canvas, the inherently flat surface that can never be the three-dimensionality world it often seeks to recapitulate.

Mythological Metaphors

Broek's research into the history of Western art has brought him to numerous classical narratives, as evidenced by canvases such as *Kill that Bastard Actaeon* (2007) and *Tarquinius and Lucretia* (2007), which bear prescriptive warnings against the dangers of voyeurism and, by extension, lust. Consistent with his interest in mythology, *Party* (2007) schematically replicates *Titian's Baccanal of the Andrians* (c.1523) and epitomizes Broek's rhetorical reconsiderations of classical culture. Loose outlines, rough edges, and a simplified palette replace the purposeful lines, careful modeling, and complex color of Titian's example. Liberated from the precision of Titian's practice, *Party's* resulting jagged bodies and floating planes of color approximate modernist precedents, simultaneously gesturing toward the geometry of Cézanne's turn-of-the-century *Bathers* and the dream-like atmosphere of Matisse's *Joy of Life* (1905-06). Moreover, Broek's reduction of Titian's image to a more intimate scale limits the image to a more select group of themes. Building on the fact that Titian's own image was itself a visual translation of an ekphrastic passage describing a gallery visit from Philostratus' *Imagines*, Broek inscribes himself into the infinitely stratified layers of artistic appropriation.

In abstracting both the form and the content of the earlier image, Broek condenses many issues into a single skeletal specter. Even the emphatically simple title *Party* confirms Broek's desire to extract what he deems the essential spirit of the artwork. But aside from alluding to the general Renaissance interest in classical antiquity and Titian's particular placement within that phenomenon, Broek's treatment of the pictorial surface asserts a theoretical claim about painting itself. The nude, exposed patches of canvas that sit amidst his patchily applied color – here perhaps most noticeably on the reclining female figure placed on the lower right-hand corner of the composition typically read as a citation of the Vatican *Sleeping Ariadne* (AD) – can be read as a metaphor for the vulnerability of both artwork and artist, always under and hence subject to the watchful eye of both critic and collector. Such a reading is underscored by a second work, *Flay that Sucker Marsyas* (2007), another improvisational intervention inspired by Titian that similarly attests to its own vulnerability on literal and metaphorical grounds as the focus of the painting and canvas itself are violently laid bare in a single pictorial gesture. Indeed recalling that a branch of the artist's family on his father's side had carried the surname Bachhus encourages acknowledging an autobiographical element in this work.

Indecent Exposures

Sex (2007) portrays a key scene from Stanley Kubrick's *Eyes Wide Shut* (1999), the focus of a growing portion of Broek's work concerned with voyeurism and the male heterosexual gaze, past and present. *Sex* draws the viewer into a world of forbidden desire where mainstream businessmen relinquish their Wall Street suits for monk-like robes and masks that obscure their public personae as they live out their orgiastic fantasies in the anachronistic architecture of a remote suburban castle. Again working with a sepia-toned palette applied in stain-like planes, Broek historicizes the narrative, whose representation oscillates between a medieval religious ritual and an elegant nineteenth-century ballroom, a notion underscored by the elegant chandelier and facemasks that recall a costume ball. These ghost-like, cloak-and-dagger masters of sex-slaves (by night)/traders (by day) hungrily consume the exposed naked bodies of the prostitutes who service them in a series of perverse rituals.

Broek's monochromatic palette creates stylistic confusion as well, conflating nineteenth-century photography with similarly toned earlier traditions of underpainting in a mistranslation of Kubrick's carefully choreographed members-only whorehouse. The cloaked businessmen, whose costumes as seen in the film itself seem utterly artificial, are here legitimated as they masquerade more convincingly as medieval monks. Above all, however, this scene pits the penetrative male gaze against the vulnerable female body, perhaps another articulation of the dynamics at work in *Party* and *The Hunt* discussed above. Another instance of hunter and prey, *Sex* grafts the inescapable plight of the artist at the mercy of the critic and, by extension, the art world onto the exposed skin of the ladies who strut and dance before their judges. While Kubrick plays on the voyeurism encouraged by the viewer who sits in obscurity in the dark movie theater, Broek inverts that energy and catches the viewer "in the act," since his image appears in the lit gallery where no viewer can remain invisible. In the end, the dynamic of production and consumption seems perhaps more perverse than any act to be performed within the walls of this strange and mysterious space.

Last Rites

Hans Broek's recent work can be read in Wölfflinian terms as a baroque counterpart to his earlier classical canvases. His production of multiple images inspired by a single source allows him to create serial meditations on single works or given themes. In this sense, one can read his collections of monads as a neo-baroque gesture replete with its own set of social and aesthetic possibilities. In producing what he himself calls "improvisations," Broek both embraces and rejects his predecessors, eliminating their authorship in an oedipal gesture that simultaneously displaces and reinforces their import as he establishes his own. These improvisational images open up – rather than close off – the possibilities of appropriative aesthetics. And so Broek's recent paintings do not simply kill off their inspiration; rather, they resurrect the energy of the past in a series of uncanny references to and reflections on the driving forces not only central to representation but also human nature itself. Thus, these new impressions stand as spectral doppelgängers that form an original archive of archetypal patterns of human behavior.

Jennie Hirsh teaches modern and contemporary art in the Department of Art History at the Maryland Institute College of Art. She holds a PhD from Bryn Mawr College, as well as an MA in Italian Studies from Middlebury College and a BA in classical studies from the University of Pennsylvania.

Close to Hans Broek

By Hugo J. Postma

I would like my work to go to a very free place where things are not limited by unnecessary rules. – Hans Broek

When do you consider a painting you make, to be finished?*

When I make something, whether or not I had planned it in my mind, and I am surprised by its power, then I can accept it as a finished work. There is always the possibility of continuing to work on an image, but I can only consider it to be finished when I can sense immediacy in the work.
I am interested in this directness...I always try to preserve the directness of a sketch. I do not attempt to "kill" the subject of my painting, to perfect the paintings, to make them a little better, or do a little more. That was something I did at times when I was working in Holland. In those days, I had to do everything again and again; my instinct was to sand the surface off once more until there was no life left in it. But I have left this tendency behind. Now I really cherish the possibility of immediacy in painting.

Can you tell me something about your working methods?

I find the images that I use in books, films, magazines and museum collections. I then usually take a photograph of the image. That makes the beginning of my process, and, from there, I make a painting based on that photograph, though I do not exactly copy it. In each case, the image that I choose holds something of great importance to me. The act of painting allows me to experience, or liberate, a particular power present in that original image.

I work in a traditional manner, on linen with oil paint. I make a sketch in burnt sienna on a light gray base; from there, I build up color that relates to the original image, but is not necessarily dictated by it. The subject of the original image is thus permitted to become a new one in my painting. For example, when I select an image from a film, this does not mean that the painting is necessarily "about" that movie. I take possession of that image and imbue it with new meaning, which exists outside the context and subject matter of the original film. The process is about identifying a metaphor that I believe exists within the image.

Why do you work with existing images that you find in films or books?

There is so much material to choose from that it becomes more a question of why you shouldn't use it, especially since images are recycled constantly and always have been recycled through different media, from painting to film, from film to photography. For example, if you take the film Barry Lyndon, you find that Kubrick used quite a few of Constable's paintings as inspiration for his scenes. There is always, and there always has been, a great deal of cross fertilization in art, from one medium to another. My images are not medium specific; this is not the sort of painting that you can see only in oil paint on linen. Rather, you can find this type of imagery in film, photography, and even theatre. What I find compelling are the exchanges that occur between different media. In my painting, I also use images drawn from Roman sculpture. I find translating from one medium to another an important component of my process, and I reserve the right to include elements that are important to me.

Based on what criteria do you choose to work with an image ?
I am searching for an undercurrent in our existence as human beings, in what distinguishes us as human. I am interested in the stories that remain with us, that reoccur, and that must be told again. Stories that have to be played out in different forms and situations by other people. Take the story of Romeo and Juliet, which is of course written by Shakespeare. This story is played out in everyday life again and again, with pairs of lovers that cannot be together, for one reason or another, and the drama of these disastrous liaisons is a universal experience.

So my painting is about this undercurrent of energy that permeates our human existence. These archetypical stories include jealousy, revenge, hubris as well as more pleasant emotions like happiness and ecstasy. I am fascinated by things that remain the same but reappear in new and unexpected forms.

Could you give an example of images that you have chosen, where they came from, and in what works you have used them? You mentioned, for instance, Barry Lyndon.
Let's talk about Titian, because he deals with the kind of energy that lies at the core of our existence, an energy that fuels very basic human drives that do not have anything to do with morality, something that occurs below the surface and is stronger than the moral structures we create. I am tapping into that undercurrent with these paintings. For instance, this painting is based on an original by Titian entitled The Death of Actaeon but I have called my version Kill that Bastard Actaeon. This is the mythological story about the hunter Actaeon stumbling across Artemis and a group of her nymphs while they are naked in their bath around her. Artemis, the goddess of both chastity and the hunt, is not pleased that he has seen her naked, so she transforms him into a stag. Once transformed, the hunter is no longer recognizable to his own dogs, who proceed to tear him apart, limb by limb. Actaeon is punished for looking. His voyeurism, even if accidental, is his crime, and I think that is a very interesting idea. And this painting is also about revenge, which often transpires in relationships between people. I like to tap into this kind of energy, this is what I aim to paint. The work on the left is also inspired by Titian. The original title is The Rape of Lucretia. I have renamed my version Tarquinius and Lucretia. This is a very violent scene in which we find a man stabbing a woman. I am interested in the translation of the emotions of this act, to deal with a victim and an aggressor, to capture and explore this powerful dynamic in my painting. Violence is something perennial and universal, and, in this case, very gendered. I think the main reason why I like to paint is because it allows me to tap into something profound. I want my paintings to be read as metaphors.

I like my paintings to be direct, rough, even unclean in a way, because I think that this represents a very honest way of painting. We like to imagine that we are perfectly in control of our lives with our computer-driven, technologically savvy world complete with electronics, beautiful cars and everything else, but basically we are still very clunky beings that really don't know how to deal with each other, or just screw things up without realizing what we have done. I like that aspect of our humanity to be in the work.

How do you work when choosing your images? How do you go about that? For instance, at a certain point you chose those images by Titian, but before choosing them, you've gone through numerous other images. What were you looking for?

It is important that images appeal to me emotionally as well as rationally. But it is the emotion that I'm most interested in. I'm after a specific dynamic.

So dynamism is an important criterion for you. So, formally speaking, this means that it is important to you that images have movement, speed, and action?

Yes.

But how should I imagine this, the process of looking at images and choosing them, imagine you start your day and you have decided that this is what you will do today: you will look for images. Do you look for a certain image before you know it exists?

That can definitely be the case, but I can also stumble upon something, since there is so much material to work with. Choosing happens quite naturally, it has to do with my mind at that moment. If something appeals to me today, this does not mean that it will still appeal to me six months from now. Actually I spend very little time searching for images. I have many images stored in my memory that I wanted to use but couldn't because I worked differently in the past, so when I started these film and Old Master improvisations, I already knew that I could work with a given movie or a given painting. This information was stored in my memory.

Can you give me some examples of images that were already stored in your memory?

Images from the film Barry Lyndon. There were particular images in that film that I knew I wanted to use. The film is an honest tale about a man who is not a hero. He is a person with visible flaws who makes mistakes. He is quite selfish and a hustler. But he is a product of fate who wanders around the world and falls into certain situations. Ultimately, he doesn't have much control over what happens to him. His life is shaped by his circumstances.

Well, if I remember correctly, he is also, at a certain point, very focused on chasing Marisa Berenson.

He falls in love with her. Yes, he wants to settle down and start a family. It's a perfectly natural thing to do.

Does he fall in love with her or with her money?

Probably more with her status than with her as a person.

But I also find Marisa Berenson to be very interesting; she is this stunning beauty married to Lord Lyndon; this delicate little old nobleman confined to a wheelchair. I find that the way Kubrick has filmed her to be incredibly impressive. I consider the scene where she moves out onto the balcony during a card game because she needs some fresh air and Ryan O'Neill follows her out to be one of the most beautiful scenes in cinema history. Then later, when they are lovers, Lord Lyndon confronts him.

Yes, yes. He speaks his famous last words, "Mister Barry, I'm the kind of person that is rather known as a cuckold than a fool" and chokes. Yes, it is a fantastic scene…

Then later on when they are married, he neglects her completely… So maybe he was after her status and money more than after her beauty?

Well, it's also possible Redmond Barry just didn't know how to have a relationship because he had been wandering most of his life.

Is there any resemblance between you and this Redmond Barry?
Maybe in the sense that I have been wandering, though my own wandering is not as extreme as his. He is a gambler. I would say that painting, in a way, is also a risk. You never know what's going to happen…you trust that you have a good deck of cards and that you will play them well. But painting is also a gamble artistically since one can never predict how people will react to the changes one makes. It's like sending a rocket into space: it costs a lot of money and you never know if and when it will find something. So I guess that art is akin to both space travel and gambling.
But, in the end, almost nothing beats obsession.

You like fast cars. For a while you even owned a Maserati. One could say that risky situations appeal to you, don't you think? Gambling, fast cars, a life that you are not sure will pay off in the end?
Yes, the idea of living a mediocre life terrifies me.

What are the personality traits and skills that you believe have helped you to cope with your life as an artist?
What helps me a lot is that I don't mind being alone. That is immeasurably important since being an artist is a rather lonely profession. You spend a lot of time being simultaneously the creator and critical audience for your work. It's really a one-man show. People who require a lot of social interaction can struggle with being an artist even if they have a lot of talent.

Does an unhappy childhood help?
I don't think that one needs to have had an unhappy childhood to be a good artist. But I think many artists, at some point or another, have been in a situation of extreme isolation, which in turn allows them to create their own reality and their own way of thinking about things. This can be quite interesting. Continuity is an another key asset. I keep going. And one has to be able to cope with rejection and failure. I think one can compare being an artist with being an explorer. Being an artist is about exploring life and, within that experience, exploring freedom.

In every life there are moments that are crucial, that determine the direction of a person's life for a number of years. Can you pinpoint any such a moment in your life?
Probably my admission to the Rijksakademie in Amsterdam was such a moment. After I finished my education at the Hogeschool voor de Kunsten in Utrecht, I entered a phase during which I painted like crazy. I had a freezing cold studio in the harbor town of IJmuiden, near Amsterdam. I had no money, and I worked as a taxi driver. Nobody was interested in my work. I applied for the Rijksakademie and was admitted. The person who really wanted to work with me was a man named Han Schuil, who is recognized as an important artist in the Netherlands. And so all of a sudden I had the opportunity to work at a wonderful school where serious people appreciated my work. This was exhilarating for me.

What made you decide to go to art school?
During high school, I was an actor in a theatre group. Some members of the group said, "Let's go to art school." And that is exactly what happened with a number of us. I had been good at drawing since I was very young, and so art school made sense for me. I enrolled in Monumental Design, which meant that I was painting full-time.

I would like to go back to your period at the Rijksakademie for a moment. Which professors, apart from Han Schuil, were

teaching you?
Well, people like Marlene Dumas, Emo Verkerk, and Jan Beutener formed the core group. And then there was this great guy from England, Bruce McLean, who always dropped in. He was a fantastic teacher with the capacity to give people a real boost of energy. Some very good work came out of those years.

What was your work in the early nineties in the Netherlands about?
It was about the mystery of ordinary things. The most ordinary things were to me the most fascinating: a house, a car, a landscape. I couldn't connect to these objects, and yet I wanted to provide reality with a recognizable image. So I would see or remember something, and, by painting it, I transformed it into a something that I could understand or feel. Through painting I could digest it, experience it.

So at that time for you painting was about digesting experiences. The paintings were neither about the actual image nor the object you depicted, but rather your connection to these objects was what the painting was about.
That's one way of putting it.

Why was it necessary at that time for you to connect to those ordinary objects?
Somehow I felt these objects were impenetrable. Painting was a means by which to connect to them. My religious upbringing as a child has made me a skeptic with a sense of mystery. I felt there was mystery in these seemingly ordinary houses, cars and landscapes.

When you left for Los Angeles in the mid-nineties your work changed and became more formal. You started to reduce images to what you have called a "formal maximum." How does that relate to the earlier, more painterly work we discussed a moment ago.
I literally eliminated paint because I didn't want people to talk about it anymore. I wasn't painting to make people enjoy brushstrokes. Linen, paint, and brushstrokes are simply a means to an end. But this so-called "end" never entered into the discourse when people would talk about my work. As a result, I started to eliminate all the surplus stuff, all the painterly effects. I wanted to get straight to the point. Imagine going to a wonderful Brahms concert and, upon returning home, saying, "Oh, I've just been to a beautiful Brahms concert, the violins had such beautiful colors and shapes." That would be ridiculous, wouldn't it? So I decided to move the violins behind the stage so that people would stop talking about the colors and shapes of my work and instead begin to listen to its music. I wanted my work to be appreciated for more compelling reasons. My Los Angeles work was about controlling the painterly medium and subject matter. This body of work clarified for me the bare essentials for making a painting. But the sense of mystery never disappeared.

You lived in Los Angeles for ten years and then two years ago you moved here to New York, where your way of working has undergone yet another dramatic shift. Why did you need this change?
Because of the ongoing reduction in my work, I began to risk losing something vital. I realized that the next stage could be only form. I wanted to inject life back into my painting, to rediscover emotion and passion. This evaluation coincided with the Columbus inside of me, as I discovered a new world, even a dark continent within myself.

Your current work is again about experiencing a part of yourself, like your work in the early nineties. But at that point it was very much about alienation and detachment as you looked out into the world and

tried to connect to it. Now you are looking inward as you try to connect with this darker side of yourself. So where do you imagine your work taking you from here? Where will it go next?

I would like my work to go to an even freer place, a place not limited by unnecessary rules. I want my work to be loose and open without being hazy or vague. I want to take it to an active place where the paintings have nothing to do with morality and instead express pure human drives, ranging from extreme violent to extreme beauty. I am searching for a place without prescriptions for "good" or "bad," but which fully acknowledges what it means to be human, in all its diversity..

Close to Hans Broek" is the transcript of an interview conducted by Hugo J. Postma on September 22, 2007 in the artist's studio in the Leviton Building in Brooklyn, New York. Postma works as a copywriter and publicist in the Netherlands. Postma studied Fine Arts in Groningen as well as Art History and Archeology in Amsterdam.

Resume

Hans Broek
Veenendaal (1965, the Netherlands)

Education and travel

2005	Moved to New York
1995 - 2005	Living in Los Angeles
1992	Travel in Russia
1991 - 1993	Rijksakademie van Beeldende Kunsten, Amsterdam, the Netherlands Post-Graduate Fellow
1983 - 1988	Hogeschool voor de Kunsten, Utrecht, the Netherlands Masters of Fine Arts, Painting

Lectures and Teaching

2007	Lecture Cooper Union, New York Lecture Guelph, Canada
2002 - 2005	Visiting professor at UCLA department of Art
2005	Lecture USC

Awards

1993	Uriot Prize, Amsterdam
1992	Royal Subsidy for Painting

Solo Exhibitions

2007	Torch Gallery, Amsterdam, the Netherlands Newman Popiashvili Gallery, New York Galerie Tanya Rumpff, Haarlem, the Netherlands Gallery Fahnemann, Berlin, Germany 'Fiction To Fiction' Artcore, Toronto, Canada
2006	Galerie Tanya Rumpff, Haarlem, the Netherlands
2005	'New work', Torch Gallery, Amsterdam, the Netherlands
2004	'Ten Years', Dordrechts Museum, Dordrecht, the Netherlands Galerie Tanya Rumpff, Haarlem, the Netherlands
2003	'Flat Air', Black Dragon Society, Los Angeles
2000	'New work', Galerie Tanya Rumpff, Haarlem, the Netherlands
1999	De Nederlandsche Bank, Amsterdam, the Netherlands
1998	Art & Project, Kunstrai, Amsterdam, the Netherlands
1997	'Hans Broek; The Open Road', De Pont Stichting, Tilburg, the Netherlands
1994	Stedelijk Museum, Bureau Amsterdam, Amsterdam, the Netherlands
1993	Art & Project, Slootdorp, the Netherlands

Group Exhibitions (a selection)

2007	'Berlin NL', Dutch Embassy, Berlin, Germany Art Cologne Palma de Mallorca, for Galeries Tanya Rumpff and Fahnemann 'Contour/Continuiteit' Contemporary Dutch Art, Museum Prinsenhof, Delft, the Netherlands

	'Too Far, Too Near' Galerie Tanya Rumpff
2006	Pulse Art Fair New York for Torch gallery
	Art Rotterdam, the Netherlands, for Tanya Rumpff
2005	ArtCologne for Tanya Rumpff and Torch galleries
	Volta, Basel for Torch Gallery
2004	'What's New' with Marlene Dumas, Vincent van Gogh and Henri Matisse, Annet Gelink Gallery, Amsterdam, the Netherlands
	'See California Now', Gallery 'C', curated by Peter Frank, Hermosa Beach
	'Heavy Duty', De Vishal, Haarlem, the Netherlands
2003	Richard Telles Fine Art, Los Angeles
	Margo Victor Gallery, Los Angeles
	Victoria Miro Gallery, London, Great Britain
2002	'Life In A Glass House', Stedelijk Museum, Amsterdam, the Netherlands
	'Contemporary Art from the Netherlands'. European Central Bank, Frankfurt, Germany
2001	Galerie Sander, Berlin, Germany
2000	'Twisted', Urban and Visionary Landscapes in Contemporary Painting, Stedelijk van Abbe Museum, Eindhoven, the Netherlands
	'There is no spirit in painting', le Consortium centre d'art contemporain, France
	'Aspekte Zeitgenossischer Kunst II', Galerie Sander, Darmstadt, Germany
1999	'Het Andere Land', Fries Museum, Leeuwarden, the Netherlands
	ArtForum Berlin, Berlin, Germany
	De Pont Stichting, Tilburg, the Netherlands
	Ferdinand van Dieten, Amsterdam, the Netherlands
1998	Kunstrai, Amsterdam for Art & Project
	Ferdinand van Dieten, Amsterdam, the Netherlands
1997	Kunstrai, Amsterdam for Art & Project
	'Gemengd Bedrijf', Art & Project, Slootdorp, the Netherlands
	Peter Stuyvesant Collectie, Amsterdam, the Netherlands
	'De keuze van de kenner', Nieuwspoort, the Hague, the Netherlands
	'Einde Eeuw, Tableau Vivant', Pulchri Studio, the Hague, the Netherlands
1996	'De Noordkaap en LA', Lumen Travo, Amsterdam, the Netherlands
	'Ver na Vermeer: Hedendaagse Schilders in Nederland en Vlaanderen', De Beyerd, Breda, the Netherlands
	'Collectie Oce -van der Grinten: Jonge Kunst 1990-1996', Bonnefanten Museum Maastricht, the Netherlands
1994	'Germinations 8' touring Breda, Warzaw, Athens, Madrid, Lisbon
1993	'Open Ateliers 1993', Rijksakademie van Beeldende Kunsten, Amsterdam
1992	Koninklijke Subsidie voor vrije schilderkunst, Royal Palace, Amsterdam

Bibliography (a selection)

2007	'Close to Hans Broek', Hugo J Postma
	'Old Faces, New Impressions' by Jennie Hirsh
2004	'De landschappen van Hans Broek', bulletin Dordrechts Museum
	'Nieuw licht in een wild landschap', De Gelderlander
	'Het ritme van de grote stad in verf', review by Paola van de Velde, de Telegraaf
	'De landschappen van Hans Broek zijn echte thrillers', het Parool, review by Jhim Lamoree

'Amerikaanse overwinning op de natuur', Rotterdams Dagblad, review by Sandra Smets
Reviews at Rijnmond.nl, galleries.nl, kunstwereld.nl
'Kunst geeft reflectie', Trouw
'L.A. in Dordrecht', Museumnieuws
'Nuchter met een vleugje mystiek', De Volkskrant, review by Marina de Vries
'Het Landschap van Hans Broek', de Dortenaar, Review by Wilko Peenstra
'Doordringen in het ondoordringbare', Haarlems Dagblad, review by Sandrine van Noord
'Alles is anoniem in Hans Broeks artificiele wereld', NRC Handelsblad, review by Janneke Wesseling
'De vondst van het eigen geluid', de Volkskrant, review by Wieteke van Zeil
'Kastanjebloesem in de Vishal', het Parool
'De innemende kracht van verf', de Volkskrant, review by Sandrine van Noort

2003 Art US, article by Tamara Sussman
The Guardian, article by Jessica Lack
Metro, review by Fisun Guner
Time Out, review by Martin Coomer
The Guardian, exhibitions pick of the week
What's on in London, review by Morgan Falconer

2002 'Life in a glass house', catalogue, Stedelijk Museum, Amsterdam
reviews in Dutch press

2001 'Unlocked', catalogue Rabobank
reviews in Dutch press

2000 'City Landscapes & Urban Landscapes', Twisted, Urban & Visionary Landscapes in ContemporaryPainting, exh. Cat. Stedelijk van Abbe Museum, Eindhoven, F.A. Hettig

1999 Lijnen, schimmen en verleidelijke kolibries', NRC Handelsblad review by H. den Hartog

1997 'Met Hans Broek loom naar Los Angeles', Trouw , review by R.Roos
'Hollywood in de Zeventiende Eeuw: Het Amerikaanse licht op de 'Hollandse schilderijen van Hans Broek', NRC Handelsblad review by Anna Tilroe
'Brandschone landschappen', Eindhovens Dagblad, review by A van der Burght
'De Pont Stichting', De Witte Raaf, review by E. Wijnants
'Hans Broek, schilder van het Californische licht. Ik voel me daar als een vis in het water', De Telegraaf, review by P.van de Velde

1996 S.N., Hans Broek', De Pont Kwartaalbericht

1995 'Hans Broek', exh. Cat Hedendaagse schilders in Nederland en Vlaanderen, articles by L. Bekkers, E. Stegeman
'De wereld onder handbereik', Metropolis M, review by Rutger Pontzen

1994 'Hans Broek', Metropolis M, review by E. Stegeman
'Galerie', NRC Hansdelsblad, review by D. Pieters
'Oefening in schijn en wezen', Nieuwsbrief Stedelijk Museum Bureau Amsterdam, article by R. Bijkerk

1993 'Herkenbare onderwerpen, laag voor laag opgebracht'. Expositie IJmuidenaar Hans Broek in Slootdorp, Noordhollands Dagblad, review by S. Postma

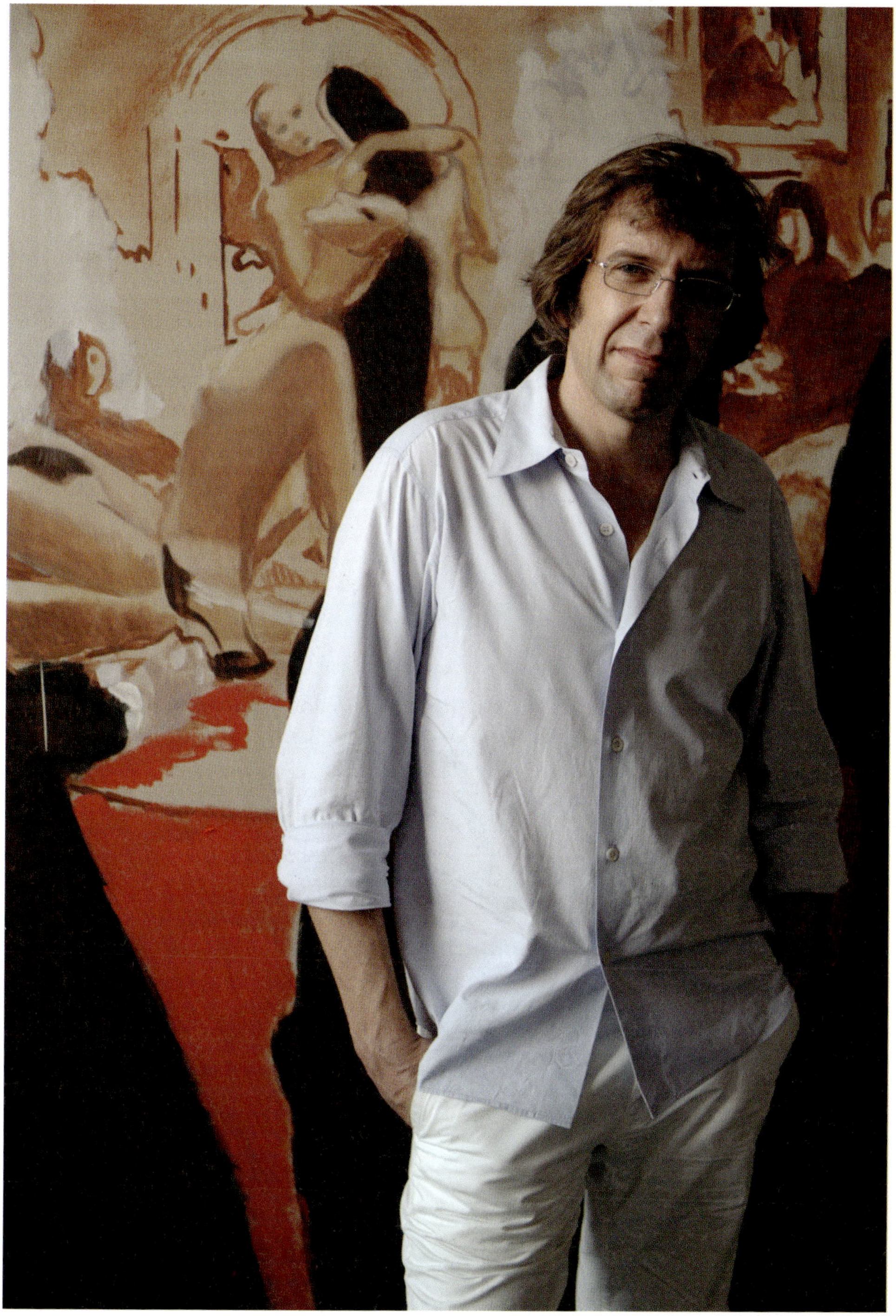

Texts
Jennie Hirsh PhD, drs Hugo J Postma

Photography
Bill Orcutt, Mark Woods
portrait: Metin Oner

Design
75B Rotterdam

Production
Sebastiaan Hanekroot

Printing
Veenman

Credits
Galerie Tanya Rumpff
Spaarnwouderstraat 74
2011 AE Haarlem
The Netherlands, t. +31 23 5359565
trumpff@xs4all.nl
www.galerietanyarumpff.nl

Newman Popiashvili Gallery
504 West 22nd Street
New York, NY 10011, t. 2122749166
www.npgallery.com
contact@npgallery.com

TORCH Gallery
Lauriergracht 94
1016 RN Amsterdam
The Netherlands, t. +31 20 6260284
info@torchgallery.com

Artcore/Fabrice Marcolini
55 Mill Street, Pure Spirit Building 62
Toronto, Canada M5A 3C4
t. +1 4169203820
mail@artcoregallery.com
www.artcoregallery.com

Galerie Fahnemann
Gipsstrasse 14
D-10119 Berlin, t. +49 30 8839897
info@galerie-fahnemann.de
www.galerie-fahnemann.de

Publisher
Veenman Publishers / Gijs Stork
Sevillaweg 140
3047 AL Rotterdam- NL
t. +31 10 245 3333 f. +31 10 245 3344
info@veenmanpublishers.com
www.veenmanpublishers.com

ISBN 978 90-8690
Copyrights

Distribution
D.A.P. 155 Sixth Avenue 2nd floor
New York, NY 10013, USA
t. +1 2126271999, dap@dapinc.com

vice versa vertrieb, Immanuelkirchstr. 12
D-10405 Berlin, t. + 49 30 61609236
info@vice-versa-vertrieb.de

Idea Books, Nieuwe Herengracht 11
1011 RK Amsterdam, t. +31 206226154
idea@ideabooks.nl

Art Data, 12 Bell Industrial Estate
50 Cunnington Street, W4 5HB London
t. +44 2087471061, info@artdata.co.uk

Special thanks to
Saskia Bos, Robert Beckand, Charlotte Dumas, Clemens Fahnemann, Dortee Farrar, Adriaan van der Have, Jennie Hirsh, Robert Kloos, Fabrice Marcolini, Marisa Newman, Irena Popiashvili, Hugo Postma, Tanya Rumpff, Gijs Stork, Mark Woods

This publication was generously supported by:
Galerie Tanya Rumpff, Newman Popiashvili Gallery, TORCH Gallery, Artcore/Fabrice Marcolini, Galerie Fahnemann

Koninkrijk der Nederlanden